# Parenting With Open Eyes

## Dr. Don N. Bacchus

**outskirts
press**

# ACKNOWLEDGEMENT

Special thanks to my wife, Roseanne, for all her love and support in writing this book. In the text, the use of the pronoun "he" in reference to the child is in no way a reflection of gender bias. It is only used for simplicity and convenience. Many important concepts in this book are repeated for emphasis and reinforcement.

# INTRODUCTION

Any person can become a parent. There are no requirements. You do not have to attend any special classes and you do not have to subject yourself to any special evaluations. As a parent you can either help your child to become an independent, productive, loving adult or you can participate in the destruction of his life. To be an effective parent you must possess knowledge and you must develop parenting skills. You must be aware of your child's functioning and you must be aware of the impact you are having on him. Your child is not here to meet your needs. Do not seek anything in return. It is your job to coach your child into becoming a mature adult. There are essential life skills that he will need to learn. As a parent, dedicate yourself to the mission of developing in your child a tremendous capacity to love.

# CONTENTS

# PREVENTION

There are two aspects to prevention. The first concern is preventing a problem from developing. The second issue is preventing a problem from getting worse. Be vigilant and invest in your child's physical and mental health. Make every effort to prevent your child from experiencing physical accidents and emotional traumas. Evaluate the possible impact of every activity on your child with an eye towards the risks and the benefits. Reduce the stress on your child so that he does not experience crippling anxiety disorder.

# MAJOR FOCUS

Your major focus as a parent is to raise a good citizen who is fully capable of independent and productive functioning. There are three targets to keep in mind. The first goal is to prevent your child from going to an early grave. This is about safety and decision making. The second goal is to keep your child from the hell of prison. This is about conscience, and self-regulation. The third goal is to keep your child from being admitted to a psychiatric hospital. This is about managing anxiety, anger, fear, and sadness. With these three goals in mind, you must teach your child essential life skills such as safety, compliance to authority, and social appropriateness. As a parent, you must teach your child to know the difference between right and wrong and help him to develop a conscience. He must learn to obey the laws of society. Your child must be able to control his impulses—especially his anger. You must teach your child to relax, and help him develop the inner strength to cope with age-appropriate demands. As a parent, you want your child to grow up to be a happy, creative, and productive person.

# SELF-IMPROVEMENT

The one best thing that you can do for your child is to become a competent parent. Work towards self-improvement. Cultivate an open mind and a willingness to learn. There is a lot that we do not know and there is a lot to learn. We do not have all the answers. Read a book on parenting. Talk to your church pastor or maybe the next-door neighbor who is raising children. Work to improve your physical and mental health. Be a good role model. Strive to become a good citizen. Know the difference between right and wrong and cultivate a conscience. Learn to be kind and loving. It is not only about what you know and what you do. It is mostly about who you are. Are you hateful and angry? Are you depressed? Do you function with heightened anxiety? Warning! If you suffer from significant mental illness, you will destroy your child. It is that simple. Your role as a parent is to facilitate your child's development as an independent, loving, and fully functioning adult.

# SOME ESSENTIAL LIFE SKILLS

The acquisition of essential life skills will make your child feel competent and confident. Some essential life skills are walking, talking, feeding himself, toilet training, using a pair of safety scissors, learning to read, basic math skills, basic writing skills, sitting still and completing an assigned task, completing a challenging task, greeting others, having a conversation, self-control, using the telephone, dressing himself, learning to take a shower, following a schedule, cooperation and team work, focus and concentration, making friends, performing household chores, safety knowledge, basic cooking skills, solving a simple problem, coping with his emotions, dealing effectively with frustration, doing laundry, organizational skills, personal healthcare, budgeting, problem solving, managing time, technology skills, making a decision, and learning to drive.

# LIMITED TIME/
# POSITIVE EXPERIENCES

To produce a happy and successful child you must expose him to many positive experiences. Life is about engaging in meaningful activities in view of limited time. As a parent, help to develop your child's creativity. Help him to learn essential life skills so that he can become competent, independent, and productive. One positive experience can have a tremendous and enduring impact on his life. Your child will not wake up one day with acquired skills. He must be taught and he must practice. There is no time to waste.

# NORMAL

Your child is unique. It is your job to discover your child and to delight yourself in his special ways. Be a keen observer. Your child may be different and yet quite normal. The definition of normal is average functioning for your child's specific age. There is a significant range that is considered to be normal. Children develop at their own rate. In some areas of functioning your child may be ahead and in some areas he may be behind. Be patient and wait for your child to mature. There is no reason to compare your child with other children. Keep in mind the concept of readiness. You can enhance your child's readiness to learn new skills by making sure he is physically healthy and by providing him with enjoyable sensory and intellectual stimulation. Do not pressure. Stress is bad for your child. If you are concerned about his rate of development, you should first talk to your child's pediatrician. You may also ask for a consultation with your local school psychologist to discuss your concerns. Should you observe rocking behaviors, head-banging, failure to respond to your voice, or excessive and prolonged crying, you should get in touch with your child's pediatrician immediately. If a developmental assessment is completed, ask the clinician whether or not your child is above average or below average. Normal is quite a large range.

# A SENSE OF SAFETY

Give your child a sense of safety and security. When he is in distress, go to him immediately and comfort him. Cuddle your baby to make him feel loved and feel connected to you. As your baby grows older, a soft light blanket will add to his comfort. Your baby will also enjoy soft, cuddly toys. When you carry your baby, hold him in a secure and safe manner close to your body. Let him feel your heartbeat and the warmth of your body. This contact comfort will make your baby feel safe, secure, and loved.

# STIMULATION

Provide a stimulating environment for your child but do not go overboard. Sensory over-load should be avoided. Allow sufficient room for your baby to kick his legs and move his arms. Your child's room should be colorful. Soft music will provide some auditory stimulation. Look at your child's face when you talk to him. Read to your child from the beginning. Let him look at large pictures. A gentle massage will feel good. You can shake a rattle from one side and then from the other side and encourage him to follow the sound. Sing songs to your child. Have him look in a mirror. Let your child enjoy the aroma coming from your kitchen. As he gets older, allow your child to experience different tastes.

# SAFETY

As a parent, commit yourself to the preservation of your child's life and to the enhancement of his health. There are many safety precautions that you must take and there are safety measures that you must teach your child. Supervise your young child at all times and especially so when he is in a risky environment. Do not allow your child to go to the driveway by himself. Never allow your child to play in the street. Keep your doors closed. Do not allow your child to be on high places. Never leave young children alone with family dogs. Never leave your child locked up in a vehicle. Transporting your child in a motor vehicle is full of risks. Be careful when you drive. Make sure the tires on your vehicle are safe and properly inflated. Make sure that everyone wears a seatbelt. In regards to food, teach your child to eat slowly to avoid choking on his food. Hot dogs are especially risky. Your child should never put inedible objects in his mouth. Make sure the water temperature in your house is low enough to prevent scalding. Always check the stove before leaving the house. Have smoke and fire detectors installed in your home and replace the batteries when needed. Do not allow your child to be near an open fire and do not allow him to play with explosives. Always have two adults in the pool when there are children present. Some bodies of water contain harmful bacteria. Be careful. A young child must never be left alone in a tub of water. A life jacket for a non-swimmer is a must. Rides in amusement parks are sometimes poorly maintained. Bunk beds are dangerous. Never sleep in a bed with an infant. Plastic bags can suffocate a child. Lock away all medications. Toys with strings can strangle. A child can fall from a shopping cart. Jumping on a trampoline is risky. Some sports are dangerous. Teach your child his family contact information and teach your child not to trust strangers. Your older child must be able to call 911 in an emergency. Your child must be taught that no one has the right to invade his personal space or touch him inappropriately. You and your child must learn to never create an opportunity to become a victim. Always be aware of your environment. At the first hint of danger, you must remove yourself to a safe place. As a parent, establish safety rules for your family and never violate them. As a parent, you need to consider the laws of probability. Home may be the safest place to be.

# IMITATION

I mitation is the most basic form of learning. Demonstrate a range of behaviors and let your child copy you. Get your child to imitate vocal sounds and movement such as clapping your hands. Have your child imitate animal sounds. Your child can also imitate you raising your arms up and putting them down. With your older child, you can have him imitate you as you walk and stop. Make it a game and make it fun. Your older child can imitate your dance moves. Have your child imitate the kind and loving words that you speak. Have your child imitate the kind acts that you perform.

# COMPLIANCE

Your child must learn to readily comply with your request. You are the parent. When you ask your child to come, he should come immediately. When you ask your child to stop, he should stop immediately. With practice, your child will learn to trust your commands and comply. Compliance practice helps to strengthen impulse control which is essential for the self-regulation of behavior. Impulse control is an essential life skill that can prevent your child from engaging in violence. Immediate compliance on a child's part is also an important safety measure. A compliant child is a teachable child who can become a great student and a good citizen.

# EARLY INDOCTRINATION

As a parent, be careful about the beliefs that you teach your child. Beliefs lead to feelings, and feelings lead to behaviors. Give your child time to mature. Consider this. Some of your beliefs may not be factual or even healthy. There will be ample time to share and discuss some of your beliefs with your child when he is an adolescent. Do not fill your young child's head with scary and unrealistic stories. Instead, by your teachings and by your example, teach your child to know the difference between right and wrong. As a parent, indoctrinate your child on the merits of kindness, love, and tolerance.

# BEDTIME

Children need at least ten hours of sleep every night. Keep your child on a consistent bedtime schedule. Make bedtime a happy time. Read a pleasant story to your child or tell him a story that teaches a positive lesson. Sing some songs. Snuggle with your child before you tuck him into bed. If your child is afraid of the dark, you can leave a night light on. Help to make your child feel safe and secure. Quality sleep is essential for your child's physical and mental health.

# STRUCTURE

Too much structure in a child's life will lead to rigidity, high anxiety, and stress. Too little structure in a child's life will make for a chaotic existence, high anxiety, and stress. A moderate amount of structure will add security and predictability to your child's life. A moderate amount of structure will lower your child's stress and still allow room for creative activities. A basic schedule for bedtime and family activities is sufficient.

# YOUR CHILD IS A CHILD

Your child is a child. Do not expose him to the concerns of adult family members. Your child does not have the brain capacity nor the life experience to cope with and process adult matters. Too much stress on your child will cause him to exhibit emotional and behavioral problems. As a parent, do not treat your child as if he is an adult companion. Do not treat your child as if he is your therapist. The physical and mental health of your child are your major responsibility. Encourage him to relax. Have him exercise and spend time in nature every day. Your child is a child. Let him enjoy his childhood and create some fond memories.

# YOUR CHILD'S DEVELOPMENT

Let your young child move his hand and leg muscles freely. Help him learn to stand and then learn to walk when he is ready. Talk to your child and encourage him to talk back to you. Your child will need to learn to feed himself. Encourage him to eat slowly to avoid choking on his food. Your child will need to be toilet trained beginning somewhere between the ages of two and three when his neurological system is developed enough for good sensation and physical control. Read to your child and have him learn to listen. When he is able to read, let him read to you. As your child gets older, teach him to sit still and complete a simple task such as coloring a picture. Keep your child on a fixed and therefore predictable bedtime schedule. Train your child to stop when you say stop and to come when you say come. Teach your child not to go to strangers. As your child becomes older, let him be responsible for a tidy room. Your older child should learn to adjust the shower water and take a shower safely. Encourage your child to be socially appropriate at all times. Demonstrate social skills to him and have him practice. Teach him to greet others. Train your child to be respectful and considerate of others. The more skills your child acquires, the more independent, confident, and effective he will become.

# INDEPENDENT THINKING

One of your major goals, as a parent, should be to raise a child who is fully capable of thinking for himself. To a significant degree, we are all products of our environment. Without realizing it, we absorb and adopt the beliefs held by our parents, teachers, and pastors. As your child grows older encourage him to ask questions. Listen to his opinions. Be tolerant of his beliefs. Coach him to be rational and to make sense. Ask him for the scientific evidence. Give him a chance to explain the reasoning behind his beliefs and opinions. Encourage your child to share his thoughts. Ask him for his advice now and then. Include your child in appropriate family conversations such as vacation plans and value his input. As a parent, it is important to let your child know that you do not have all the answers and that there is a lot that we do not know. Encourage him to think for himself and to live by rational ideas.

# TEMPERAMENT

As your child grows, his true temperament will be revealed. Your child may be outgoing or he may be reserved. If you have an extroverted child on your hands, you should encourage him to relax, slow down, and remain calm. Encourage your extroverted child to speak in a soft tone of voice and remind him not to engage with strangers. If you have an introverted child on your hands, you should encourage him to be more expressive and socially involved. Engage him in daily conversations. Allow him to express his thoughts and his feelings. Your reserved child will benefit from exposure to comedy. Let him learn to tell some jokes and encourage him to do some acting.

# SELF ACCEPTANCE

It is sometimes easier to admire others than to love and value ourselves. As a parent, it is your job to respect and praise your child for his ability and for his effort. Point out his uniqueness. Everyone is different. There is no need for comparison. Encourage your child to accept himself for who he is. It is important for him to understand his strengths and weaknesses. Encourage your child to value and love himself. Self-hate is destructive. Love your child. Tell him that you are proud of him and that you love him. Your child needs to know that he is special. He does not have to earn your love. Love him no matter what. If you love and value your child, he will learn to love and value himself.

# THE GIFT OF CONSCIENCE

Give your child the gift of conscience. Teach him to know the difference between right and wrong. Teach him to be socially appropriate. In a gentle manner, correct your child when it is necessary. As a parent, model appropriate social behaviors for your child. Put him through the physical practice of good behaviors. Praise his gentle and compassionate ways. Do not tolerate violence or cruelty toward pets or people. If your child shares with you that he experiences persistent thoughts to hurt animals or people, you should seek professional help for him. Allowing your child to pet a small, gentle animal will teach him to be kind. When your child is mean and unkind, give him a time out. Have him sit on a chair by himself for ten minutes. Ask him to sit quietly and feel badly for his bad behavior. Tell your child shame on your bad behavior. You should not shame your child. You should shame your child's bad behavior. A measure of shame will instill in your child a measure of guilt which will serve to build his conscience.

# TRAUMA

As a parent, one of your major jobs is to protect your child from physical and emotional trauma. Keep his environment safe and teach him safety measures. Always respond to your child's cry and provide comfort and cuddling. If your child has to be hospitalized, arrange to stay with him. All medical procedures that are not urgent should be postponed until your child is older. Never throw a young child into a swimming pool to teach him to swim. Never force your child to interact with friends or family members. Explain storms to your older child. Relocation or divorce are traumatic. Protect your child from scary people and scary situations. Do not introduce frightening topics to your young child. Do not expose him to scary videos. You want to raise a mentally tough and resilient child, but you do not want to raise a frightened child. Be determined to keep the traumas to your child at a minimum. Strive to make him feel safe and protected at all times.

# EXERCISE

As a parent, outdoor exercise is one of the most beneficial habits you can help your child to develop. It is often the cure for many ailments. Daily vigorous exercise will enhance your child's physical and mental health. Your child will be physically stronger and he will become a better sleeper. He will also be more positive. His coping skills will be enhanced. Through outdoor exercise your child will develop a fondness for the natural world. Exercise will become a wholesome passion, and a pastime, that will bless your child for a lifetime. He may become interested in hiking or running. Exercise will be an activity that will bring great joy to your child. Encourage him to make exercising in nature a daily habit. Give your child the wonderful gift of developing a healthy addiction to daily exercise.

# STRESS

L ife is full of unavoidable stress. Some challenges are internal and some challenges are external and sometimes beyond our control. The bottom line is that stress is destructive. Protect your child from excessive stress. Your child will become strong from normal challenges and meaningful frustration. It is meaningless frustration that is damaging. Make sure what you ask of your child is age appropriate and within his range of ability. Your child must learn to complete challenging and sometimes boring tasks. Encourage him to seek the help of adult family members when help is needed but do not cultivate weakness and dependency. A fundamental goal of parenting is to raise an independent and resilient child. Your child should take some time each day to play and relax. Playing a sport or going for a walk are great distractions that reduce stress. Do not over-schedule your child. Help him to experience a sense of control and help him to feel effective in his life. As a parent, it is important to know the signs of stress such as poor sleep, violent outbursts, and body tension. In regards to stress, we can spend our time analyzing life or we can spend our time living life. Plan joyful activities for your child. Live by this mantra – "I can handle whatever comes my way."

# IMPULSE CONTROL

As your child gets older, he should learn to effectively deal with his urges and impulses. He may have an urge to move and touch. He may have an urge to hit someone. He may have an urge to run across the street. He may have an urge to speak ill of a friend or family member. Your child must develop the ability for impulse control. The more he practices, the easier it will be to control his behaviors. Take the time to teach your child to stop when you ask him to stop. Then, allow him to practice stopping upon his own command to stop. This internal control system is essential for self-regulation. There are many people in prison today because they lacked impulse control. As a parent, have your child practice impulse control daily. Soon it will become a habit.

# RIGIDITY

A child will likely be rigid if his parents are rigid. As a parent, do not claim to know everything because there is a lot that we do not know. In the absence of facts, we have beliefs. Everyone's beliefs deserve a measure of consideration. Rigidity of beliefs can lead to intolerance. Instead of saying that you are right, state and explain your belief. You may have scientific evidence for some of your beliefs. When you state a belief, you should at least have a rationale for that belief. Everyone is entitled to their opinions. Always be willing to learn from others and strive to be flexible. Do not think of yourself as morally superior. You are not the owner of absolute truth. Do not become a slave to rules and control. Do not attempt to remake another person in your image. Live your life according to rational and reasonable principles. Rigidity will add stress to your child's life. Flexibility and tolerance will improve your child's mental health and enhance his social relationships.

# AWARENESS

Increased awareness is achieved when you are observant. There are two layers to awareness. The first level of awareness involves your own functioning. Tune in to how you are feeling. Are you energized and focused? Are you aware of your emotions and your thoughts? Are you happy or sad? Is your energy high or low? Are you mentally sharp or are you experiencing brain fog? The other level of awareness involves your environment. Be aware of your environment. Is there anyone in your environment who represents a threat? Be aware of the weather conditions. Are you at risk? Coach your child into becoming more aware of his internal functioning and more aware of his environment.

# MUSIC

Music can be stimulating, comforting, or joyful. Surround your child with both soothing and rhythmic music. Your child can tap out simple rhythms on a drum pad. As your child becomes older, allow him to participate in both listening to and producing music. The natural world is rhythmic and musical. Allow your child to spend time in nature. As your child gets older, encourage him to learn to play a musical instrument. Music is a universal language that connects people from all regions of the earth. Help your child to appreciate the music that originates from different cultures. As a parent, it is important to be aware of the lyrics that your child is exposed to for there is a message in every song.

# MANAGE YOUR ANXIETY

Teach your child to manage his anxiety. If he can keep his anxiety level low, many aspects of his life will fall into place. Children begin to develop high anxiety as they become aware of death, danger, and the demands of society. The accumulation of good and usable skills will lead to feelings of competence and confidence, and serve as a buffer against anxiety. The acquisition of essential life skills will help to make your child feel effective living in the real world. As children learn to self-evaluate and self-regulate, their anxiety level will drop. As a parent, encourage your child to live in the present. Do not worry too much about the future. Many of the things that we worry about never happen. Take life one day at a time. Teach your child to relax and to use positive self-talk to structure and guide his life. Daily physical exercise and quiet time are a must. Make sure what you ask of your child is not beyond his ability level. A daily schedule will add predictability to your child's life and serve to reduce his anxiety. If, as a parent, you are experiencing high unmanaged anxiety, your child will become highly anxious too. Mild anxiety enhances performance but severe anxiety interferes with rational thinking and task completion.

# GOALS

As a parent, introduce the idea of setting goals to your older child. Be flexible and be sure to obtain input from your child. Do not have too many goals. Have a few short-term goals and a few long-term goals. When you set goals, you are creating a road map for success that reflects your values. Some short-term goals for your child can be the improvement of his grades, playing a team sport, playing a musical instrument, or starting an exercise program. Some long-term goals for your older child can be learning to drive, graduating from high school, or making a career choice. When your child has well defined goals, he will be more focused and more determined. You and your child will be better able to measure progress when you have established goals.

# BOUNDARIES

Teach your child to respect the privacy, the personal boundaries, and the property of other people. Insist that your child behave in socially appropriate ways. Teach him social behaviors through your words and through your physical demonstrations. Be firm and be consistent with behavior management. Teach your child to keep his hands to himself. There is no justification for the use of violence. Encourage your child to disagree or complain using his words. Your child can argue his case, but he should never allow his argument to escalate into physical violence. Your child should never bully others. Your child must learn to respect the personal space of other people.

# LOVE IS WHAT YOU DO

Love is not what you say. Love is not what you think. Love is what you do. Love is not effortless. Love is effortful. From the beginning, tell your child often that he is loved. Call him by his name or call him love. Every time you tell your child that you love him, touch him. Give him a kiss on the cheek or give him a gentle hug. At the very least, touch your child right after you tell him that you love him. Talk is cheap. In the end, it is what we do that counts. Love is not measured in words. Love will always be measured in terms of the effort you make for the benefit of another. Love is what you do.

# HOME EDUCATION

Teachers are trained to teach. A parent is a parent. There is no guarantee that a parent is capable of being their child's teacher. It can be confusing to a child when his parent switches from being his parent to being his teacher. Some parents home school their children because of school bullying, school shootings, or the perceived detrimental influence of other pupils. Maintaining a child in regular education is challenging for any parent. It is hard work to get a child to bed on schedule and to get him up at a set time for regular school. Regular education may involve the payment of tuition, transportation, school lunches, and parent-teacher conferences. It is important for you, the parent, to consider the benefits of enrolling your child in regular education. Your child will mature from spending some time away from you. He will learn from his interactions with his classroom teacher and his classmates. Your child will learn to develop his social skills, his coping skills, and his problem-solving ability. He will learn a great deal from observing others. In regular education your child will learn to follow a schedule and he will be exposed to a full range of curriculum subjects. As a parent, if you choose to home school your child, make sure that your home education program covers a full range of subjects. Make sure that you provide many social opportunities for your child.

# FRUSTRATION

Your child will develop inner strength and resiliency from exposure to mild to moderate meaningful frustration. Your child will learn a great deal when he faces challenges. Do not hesitate to tell your child, "No" when such a response is appropriate. Meaningful frustration includes activities such as household chores, music practice, daily exercise, social skills training, and going to bed on schedule. On the other hand, meaningless frustration is stressful and detrimental to your child. Peer group bullying is meaningless frustration. Over-scheduling your child is meaningless frustration. A physical task that is clearly beyond your child's ability level and physical strength is meaningless frustration. Exposing your child to concerns over which your child has no control is meaningless frustration. Exposing your child to adult matters is meaningless frustration. Yelling at your child and threatening him is meaningless frustration. As a parent, help your child to become mentally tough by exposing him to a moderate amount of meaningful frustration.

# FOLLOWING A SCHEDULE

F ollowing a daily schedule is an essential life skill. Teach your child to live in blocks of time. It is part of time management. Schedules are indicative of what's important to a family and specifically to a child. A schedule adds predictability to a child's life and therefore reduces stress and anxiety. Following a daily schedule is great preparation for adult living.

# WORK AND PLAY

Work and play are the two main human activities. Encourage your child to always get his work done before he plays. It is a responsible and decent way to live. Never have dessert before dinner. Teach your child to delay gratification. Let play be the just reward for being creative and productive. Schedule play after the work is completed. Many people work too much and play too little. As a parent, help your child to establish a healthy balance between work and play. This is good preparation for adult living. As a parent, cultivate a wholesome philosophy of life that incorporates the concepts of creativity, productivity, joy, and relaxation.

# LET'S GO OUTSIDE

There is something magical and therapeutic about interacting with the natural world. The great outdoors will expose you to the sights and sounds of nature. There is a certain rhythm. Some days you feel a gentle breeze and on other days the gentle breeze gives way to a gusty wind. The clouds are ever changing. Often there is wildlife to observe. Spend time in nature with your child. Plant a garden. Enjoy the sun and welcome the rain. Breathe some fresh air. Let your child learn to appreciate the peacefulness of the natural world. Let him learn to be one with nature. Take your child for a hike in the great outdoors. As you walk, let your child hug a tree and feel what it is like to be strong.

# LOVINGKINDNESS

Model kindness to your child. Be gentle in your approach to others. Be kind to yourself. You will be blessed when you share what you have. Be generous. The good feelings that come with sharing will enhance your mental health and add to your happiness. The only time you should not be kind is when you are defending yourself from an attack. Practice kindness and it will become a habit. Everyone benefits from kindness – the giver of kindness, the receiver of kindness, and the observer of kindness. If you combine love and kindness, you have the word lovingkindness. What a beautiful word!

# CHOICE

No matter the situation, you have a choice. You can choose to engage or you can choose to walk away. You can choose war or you can choose peace. You can choose your activities. You can choose your friends. You can choose to live a meaningful life or you can waste your existence and contribute nothing much to planet earth. You can choose to be miserable or you can find ways to be fulfilled and happy. At the very least, you can choose your attitude.

# POWER OF INTELLIGENCE

Intelligence is the ability to think and reason. Never underestimate the power of good intelligence. You do not have to be a genius. You can grow in intelligence. Stay physically healthy, and get adequate sleep and proper relaxation. Eat nutritious foods and drink pure water. Exercise every day. Read as many books as you can that are written at a challenging level. Engage in conversations with bright people. Keep an open mind to new ideas. Always try to be rational and always try to make sense. Practice defining problems and work towards developing solutions to problems. Be a divergent thinker. Brainstorm about all the possibilities. Be tolerant. Realize that there are many things that we do not know. Create some new ideas. Good intelligence is one of the best tools that you can use to negotiate real life.

# WILLINGNESS TO SUFFER

To live in the world is to experience physical and mental suffering. As a parent, do all that you can to relieve your suffering and the suffering of your child. Learn to accept the portion of life's suffering that cannot be resolved. A willingness to suffer will free up the energy you were wasting fighting your emotions. Life's suffering comes to us in many forms. We may have to endure losses. Our feelings may be hurt when others offend us. Cultivate the inner strength to bear your physical and mental pain. By so doing, you will be prepared to bear the pain of others. Be a good sufferer. Teach it to your child.

# CREATIVITY

Humans are on this earth to be creative and productive. Nurture your child's creativity. Let your child express himself. At a young age, get him into finger-painting. Give him some choices. Learn to be non-direct with your child. Offer hints instead of barking commands. Be a good coach. Encourage your child to make something even if it is a mud pie. An older child can color pictures or engage in sketching of a tree or an animal. Share ideas with your child. Provide materials for him that will stimulate his imagination. Engage him in storytelling. Creative experiences will enhance your child's mental, physical, and emotional growth. Creative experiences will also enhance your child's ability for divergent thinking and problem-solving.

# GET UP AND DANCE

Dancing is a form of meditation that integrates the mind and the body through rhythm and movement. Do not underestimate the power of music and dance. Dancing will keep you physically fit. Dancing will bring you joy. Dancing will enhance your body image. Dancing is a way to participate in the rhythm of the universe. Dancing will lift your depression and help to make you less inhibited. Dancing will reduce your stress and anxiety, and help you to relax. Dancing is good for your brain. Dance in private or dance in public. Dance to any music you like. Keep the rhythm alive. Let your child get up and dance.

# VIOLENCE

Violent behaviors may be caused by brain malfunction. Violent behaviors may also be connected to rage from a past traumatic event. For some, violence is a learned response that has become habit. In some families, there are no well-defined boundaries and family members have little regard for privacy. They often interact in impulsive and aggressive ways. As a parent, cultivate a family climate that is calm and respectful. Be alert to sadistic tendencies in your child. Cruelty towards animals is especially significant. Train your child to be reflective and peaceful. Encourage him to use his words to express his frustration and anger. Help him to cultivate a sacred regard for all life. Train your child to be aware of his urges to act out. Help him to develop conscience and impulse control through daily practice. Your child must first learn to stop himself upon the command of his parents. Next, he must learn to stop himself upon his own command. Self-regulation is an essential life skill. As a parent, you may wish to eliminate toy guns and violent video games. Encourage your child to be kind and peaceful. Encourage your child to be tolerant of people who have different beliefs. Help your child to be kind and caring towards people who look different. By precept and by example teach your child to be loving. It will only take seconds to go from rage to violence which can land your child in prison. Train your child to walk away and to never allow a disagreement to escalate into violence. Humans form habits easily. If you practice peacefulness, you will soon become a peaceful person.

# RHYTHM

The universe is filled with rhythm. We are rhythmic when we walk and we are rhythmic when we talk. We are rhythmic when we play music and when we play sports. We are involved in rhythm when we write poetry or when we write prose. We are rhythmic when we eat. Rhythm reduces stress and enhances our efficiency and productivity. The natural world is filled with rhythm. There is day and there is night. There is sunrise and there is sunset. There are tides and there are seasons. Our hearts beat with rhythm and our brain cycles with rhythm. From an early age, surround your child with rhythm. A place to start is with music and dance.

# EARLY SPECIALIZATION

As a parent, help your child to develop a wide range of essential life skills. Your child does not need to focus on any specific career goal at an early age. From the start, teach him the skill of compliance. Let him learn to sit still and complete a task. Have him follow a schedule. Help your child to acquire self-care skills. Teach him to be socially appropriate and to respect privacy and boundaries. Expose your young child to art, music, and science. Give him a broad foundation. Help him to explore his interests and passions. Coach him into becoming a good student who is competent in many subject areas. There is no need for early specialization.

# TECHNOLOGY

Today's world is full of technology which has increased our knowledge, our productivity, and our ability to communicate. However, with the era of computers, humans may now experience information overload which can cause confusion and stress. There is no path of escape. Help your child to become competent with technology but do not allow him to become addicted to technology. Enjoy all good things in moderation. Children should be properly supervised when using the computer. They should not be exposed to adult material. In today's world, many children experience more interactions with their cell phones than with other children. Many children are becoming robotic and socially incompetent. Many children are becoming house-bound when they could be spending time walking in nature. Do not allow technology to dominate your child's life. Do not allow your child to become a victim of internet crime. Do not allow your child to be bullied on social media. Encourage your child to read and to spend time with his friends. Get your child in the habit of getting daily exercise in the great outdoors.

# MOTOR SYSTEM DEVELOPMENT

Your child's motor system is what facilitates speech articulation as well as fine and gross motor performance. Skills such as handwriting, walking, and running are dependent on proper motor system development. Bowel and bladder control are also dependent on adequate motor system development which typically is in place by age three. Give your infant sufficient space to kick his legs and wave his arms. With time he will babble and then try to talk and walk. Allow him to safely practice. Get your young child into the habit of getting some daily exercise in the fresh air. Motor system development is also important for impulse and emotional control and should not be taken lightly. As a parent, you can strengthen your child's motor system through daily exercise and motor activities such as walking on a straight line or walking on a low, safe balance beam. You can also have your child practice speeding up when he walks, and stopping himself first on your command and then on his own command.

# VISUAL SPATIAL DEVELOPMENT

Humans are highly visual creatures. Most people become strong visual learners as they get older. There are many children who learn best through the visual system. Many of these children have difficulty with auditory learning. The comprehension of spoken language is often a problem. Provide a wealth of visual stimulation for your child. Create a bright and colorful environment for your infant. As your child gets older, teach him to point out pictures. You can strengthen his visual memory through practice. First, you show your child a picture. Then, you hide the picture. Ask him to recall the picture that he was shown. Encourage your child to form pictures in his mind when he hears a story, when he reads, and when you read to him. Visual reasoning involves the application of logical reasoning to visual patterns. Parents and teachers should work hard to develop every child into a powerful visual learner who is skilled at visual recall. Whatever your child hears may not linger for a long time in his ears. Whatever your child sees will linger in his mind's eye like a movie for a long time. Visual learning will lower your child's anxiety level and at the same time improve his overall behavior and academic achievement.

# LANGUAGE DEVELOPMENT

R ead to your baby and talk to your baby even before he is born. At a young age, let your child become familiar with the activity of reading and with having human conversations. You can introduce phonetic skills to your child as early as one year old. Explain the meaning of new vocabulary words and abstract concepts to your older child. Help your child to build his language comprehension by listening to a story and then answering questions about the story. After reading a story to your older child, ask him to tell you the story that was read to him. Engage your child in daily conversations. Have him ask and answer questions. Let your older child participate in discussions and debates that are age appropriate. Ask him for his advice and opinions on a range of family topics. The ability to understand and use language is a good indication of your child's level of intelligence.

# SEPARATION FROM PARENTS

M any children experience separation anxiety when they are away from their parents. Home is their place of safety and especially so when their parents are present. The overall goal of human development is, however, to gradually separate from your parents and become an independent and fully functioning adult. It is a sad process for everyone involved. There are many essential life skills that your child will have to acquire before he can become independent. Childhood is a preparation for adulthood. There will be many occasions when your child will be forced to be away from his parents. Attending regular school is such an occasion. As a parent, you have to trust your child's teacher to take care of your child. Children benefit greatly from time away from their parents when the parents are less than competent. Time spent away from parents serves to weaken the bonds of dependency and will help your child to mature and become strong and independent. During time away from his parents, your child will experience the workings of the real world and learn to cope with a range of social situations and challenges. In short, your child will learn to grow up.

# PROCESS AND OUTCOMES

L ife is both process and outcome. Invest in the process and the outcome will take care of itself. Give meaning to the process. Enjoy the little steps that will eventually get you to the outcome. The interactions between family and friends while fixing the Thanksgiving dinner are just as meaningful as feasting on the dinner when it is all prepared. Enjoy planting your seeds, watering your plants, and removing the weeds as you wait for harvest time. When you focus on the process, you learn to live in the present. When you live in the present your stress will be reduced. Do not try to control the process of life. Give your best effort and accept the outcome. Observe the process of life and enjoy the rhythm. Allow yourself to be fascinated by life's many surprises and the small steps that will take you to the outcome. Put effort into the process and you will have meaningful outcomes. Enjoy the ride and the scenery on your way to your destination.

# CONSTRUCT SYSTEM/
# DESTRUCT SYSTEM

Living in the real world, you can either choose to be a construct system or a destruct system. You can either be on the side of goodness or you can be on the side of evil. You have a choice. At times you will experience the urge to be kind, caring, and tolerant. Get in the habit of fulfilling this urge. There will be times when you experience the urge to be mean, revengeful, and intolerant. Get in the habit of resisting this urge. Do not allow negative emotions to dominate your life. If your negative emotions and urges are intense and overwhelming, you may wish to seek professional assistance. Engage yourself in positive self-talk and always strive to be a construct system. Teach this philosophy to your child.

# EARLY INDOCTRINATION

W hen you come into the world, you are at the mercy of the people that surround you. Whatever they tell you is what you believe. Your parents, your pastors, your teachers, and your church leaders will be the most influential. The information they provide may or may not be accurate, rational, or useful. As your child grows older, he should begin to review his early indoctrination. Many people have been told that some cultures are inferior. Many people have been told that some innocent and fun activities such as dancing are a sin. Many people have been told that sex is bad and that a punitive God will send bad people to hell. Engage in some rational thinking and then ask for the evidence. When you become an adult, it is your responsibility to reevaluate your indoctrination. Get your facts straight. You may have to change some of your beliefs. In the end, you will become less anxious and less guilty after a review of your early indoctrination. Be a courageous and progressive parent. Help your older child to review his early indoctrination. Encourage him to think for himself and to question what was taught to him. Encourage your child to adopt beliefs that are rational and evidence based. There is a lot that we do not know.

# RELAXATION

As a parent, teach your child to slow down and relax. Have your child lie on a blanket daily for ten minutes of quiet time. People can relax through exercise, slow deep breathing, and listening to soothing music. Some people think too much. Some people jump ahead to the future instead of living in the present. Some people have too much to do. Focus on the here and now. What is the weather like today? How am I feeling today? Get outside. Look at the clouds and the trees. Feel the gentle breeze. Relaxation is much more than resting. Set aside the clutter from your mind. Let your mind be calm. Count your blessings. Release the tension and the worry. Have confidence in yourself that you will be able to handle whatever comes your way. Accept the reality of life. There is much that we cannot control and there is a lot that we do not know. Teach your child to slow down and relax. Have him practice relaxation every day. Have him use his silent inner language to say the word "relax" to himself. With time his body will learn to obey.

# CONCENTRATION

The ability to attend, focus, and concentrate can be improved through daily practice. From an early age, train your child to sit still and complete a given task. Praise him for his ability to concentrate. Teach your child to listen to instructions and train him to be compliant. Good physical health, which includes proper sleep, is conducive to the development of good concentration ability. Teach your child to use self-talk as a strategy to improve his concentration. Train him to use his inner language to remind himself to concentrate. Do not get into the habit of multi-tasking. Live in blocks of time and attend to one task at a time. Do not over-schedule. Spend time outdoors and interact with nature. Be observant. To help build his concentration, have your child practice recalling pictures, letters, and numbers that were shown to him. In addition, have your child recall a series of random numbers that were recited to him. Have your child practice daily relaxation. It will improve his concentration.

# SELF-EXPRESSION

L et your child speak. Encourage him to express himself by using his words. Let him share his thoughts, his feelings, and his beliefs. Allow your child to agree and allow him to disagree. Let him express himself. Let him find release for his inner tension. As a parent, model self-expression to your child. Share your thoughts, feelings, and beliefs. Encourage your child to express himself through activities such as music, art, sports, and writing. Your child will integrate new learning with old learning when he participates in daily conversations. His social skills will also be enhanced. Through self-expression, your child will grow in confidence and creativity. Through self-expression, your child will make strides towards independent functioning. Self-expression is a form of therapy.

# INTUITION

Pay attention to the still small voice within you. The gut feeling or the hunch that you experience is your wise mind speaking to you from past experience and accumulated knowledge. Allow the wisdom of your intuition to help guide you. Some have defined intuition as keen perception or insight. Cultivate your sensible intuition. Persistent and sensible impressions are not to be ignored. The more you obey your sensible intuition, the more powerful and useful your intuition will become. On some occasions, your intuition may not be loaded with logic, but the wisdom of your mind may save your life. Your intuition will become more realistic as you dedicate yourself to discerning reality. Teach your child to trust his sensible intuition.

# DEATH

Death is a horrible word that describes a horrible reality. We will all die. We have limited time. All our relationships are therefore temporary relationships. About the age of nine, your child will begin to realize that death is permanent. At such a young age, your child will not be able to properly process the event of death. Many adults struggle to fully comprehend death. Losing a loved one will be a major traumatic experience for your child. Life is a journey. Many will drop out from the walk that we call life. Those who are left behind must walk on. After your child becomes aware of death, he may become fearful of his own death and fearful of the death of his parents and siblings. As much as possible, stay healthy and stay safe. Value life. On the other hand, none of us should allow ourselves to become imprisoned by the reality of death. Much of life is about calculated risks, counting the cost, respecting the laws of nature, and respecting the laws of probability. It is the fact of death that gives real meaning to life which really is about limited time and the use of time. Live a meaningful and productive life. Make death your friend. May death gently ride upon your shoulders to remind you moment by moment that life is a precious gift. Teach it to your child.

# COMPETENCE

As a parent, help your child to develop a range of essential life skills. It is competence that leads to confidence. Encourage your child to become an expert in his area of interest. When your child is good at what he does his sense of self will greatly improve. A solid education will provide your child with options and at the same time it will increase his confidence. A child with a range of essential life skills will develop self-respect and he will gain the respect of others. As a parent, help your child to develop his social skills, his physical skills, his technology skills, and his academic skills. A competent child will be a confident child who is well able to live his life with effectiveness.

# SCHOOL SHOOTINGS

There was a time when schools were regarded as a safe haven. It is hard to believe that anyone would go to a school and shoot children. It is equally hard to believe that our government cannot prevent it from happening. It is a sad commentary on the level of violence in our country. It also calls into question just how much children are valued. Many parents are now afraid to send their children to school. Many children are now afraid to attend school. Many teachers are fearful that a shooter will show up at any time. The anxiety level of parents, teachers, and students is at an all-time high. We should not have to put our students through drills at school in preparation for a shooter. What do we say to our children? As a parent, be open to your child's questions. Find out what your child already knows and clarify information as necessary. Give proper consideration to the age and maturity of your child. Keep routines as normal as possible and encourage him to share his concerns. Know the security plan that your child's school has in place. School shooting is a reality that will raise the anxiety level of parents, teachers, and students.

# SELF-DEFENSE

Never create an opportunity for you or your loved ones to become a victim. Think prevention. As much as possible engage in your activities during daylight hours. Be aware of your environment at all times. Park in well lighted areas as close as possible to the entrance of an open business. Have a code word such as "run" to signal danger. There are evil people in the world. Be realistic but not paranoid. As much as humanly possible, do not allow anyone to take you away from the scene and have control over you. Be prepared to fight for your life. Do not project yourself as weak and afraid. Carry yourself with confidence at all times. Do not live your life in fear.

# YOUR CHILD'S CERTAINTY

B e your child's certainty. Let your child know that you love him unconditionally and that you will be there for him no matter what the circumstances. Let him know that you are his certainty – someone he can fully trust and someone from whom he can borrow strength. Let your child know that he can always count on you when help is needed. Do not underestimate the importance of this attachment. Having a certainty in life is like having an anchor. Having a certainty means that your child will look to the future with reduced anxiety and with enhanced confidence. A good grandparent can also be your child's certainty. Let your child know that you are his certainty.

# NEGATIVE EMOTIONS

Negative emotions include fear, anxiety, sadness, jealousy, and anger. Help your child to quickly identify the negative emotion that he is experiencing. Encourage him to label his feelings and express himself. Let him know that it is normal to experience negative emotions and tell him that feelings change and change quite often. Encourage your child to remain in control. Let him know that he should not be afraid of his emotions. They are the real and rich part of our functioning. Positive as well as negative emotions make us human. Help your child to determine the trigger for his emotional response. Help him to use effective self-talk to manage his negative feelings. Coach your child into using activities such as exercise and music to help reduce his negative feelings. Encourage him to walk away from conflict. Your child must learn to deal with fear in a rational manner. He must learn to relax and think. Train your child to live in the present and to count his blessings. Encourage your child to engage in activities that make him happy. Teach your child to be kind and generous. It is important for your child to cultivate a high regard for personal space and social boundaries. We always have a choice. At the very least we can choose our attitude and the way we respond. Good choices will soon become habit. Your child should never displace his anger on to others. Physically striking someone is against the law unless it is in self-defense. Many people are in prison today because they were not able to control their rage. Guide your child into becoming the master of his negative emotions. If he does not control his negative emotions, his negative emotions will take control of him. Instill in your child a tremendous capacity to love. You do this by loving your child and by being a great example of love.

# MENTAL ILLNESS

Mental illness is experienced when your mind is stressed and there is impairment in your thinking, your mood, or your behavior. Brain deficits or emotional trauma are often root causes. The most common mental illnesses are high anxiety, phobias, depression, and rage. Mental illness is treatable by medication and by psychotherapy. Mental illness can be placed on a continuum of mild, moderate, and severe. Counseling is regarded as a non-drastic intervention for mental illness while medication and hospitalization are regarded as extreme interventions. As your child gets older, let him know that his mental health is as important as his physical health. A person's mental health may be enhanced through proper nutrition, quality sleep, daily exercise, social contact with good friends and family, rational thinking, and participation in joyful activities. In some cases, people who are mentally ill have no awareness that they are mentally ill. As a parent, teach your child about self-evaluation for it is a prerequisite to any type of self-regulation. A person's mental health can change over time. As a parent, work hard to cultivate your own mental health so that you can have a positive impact on your child.

# RACISM

Let us share the planet and live together in peace. I am not superior to you and you are not superior to me. I am not inferior to you and you are not inferior to me. I may look different but I am human with the same human qualities as you. I get hungry and I get scared just like you. Internalize the idea that all people are of equal value. Do not practice racism in any shape or form and do not plead racism when you have been irresponsible or when you have broken the law. Value everyone equally. Be fascinated by racial and cultural differences. Racism keeps people apart and hinders us from taking care of each other. Rid your mind of this evil. Treat everyone with dignity and with respect. What a person looks like is irrelevant. It is a man's character that matters. When you interact with others, do not consider their race. View them as people. As a parent, if you are a racist, your child will become a racist. Cultivate an open mind that is full of love. Seek out social interactions with people of all races. Teach love, kindness, and toleration to your child. Be a good example. Cuddle a baby of every race! These same precious cuddly babies grow up to be adults.

# TRUTH

The truth will make you free. Tell the truth and live the truth. Do not lie to others and do not lie to yourself. Your sins will find you out. Live truthfully and you will have little for which to apologize. When you tell the truth and when you live the truth, your anxiety level will be greatly reduced. Whether it is a small matter or a large matter, make it a life-long habit to tell the truth. Tell the truth about yourself to yourself. Be a good person and speak the truth. Be a good example for your children. In the end, in every situation, truth is in everyone's best interest. Of course, you should lie to save your life and the life of others if confronted by a criminal who is about to do you and others harm. One layer of truth, sometimes referred to as provable or absolute truth, consists of facts supported by scientific evidence. Another layer of truth is the beliefs that you have chosen to own as your personal truth. Personal truth is often a mixture of opinions, feelings, and beliefs. You may wish to share your personal truth, but never try to impose your personal truth on others. Keep in mind that your personal truth may not be backed up by scientific evidence.

# RATIONAL THINKING

By nature, humans are more emotional than rational. It is our emotions that get us in trouble most of the time. If you are going to live a successful life, you must dedicate yourself to the principle of being rational. Strive to always make sense and stay grounded in reality. This approach will make you mentally strong. When you are rational, your coping and problem-solving skills will dramatically improve. Train your child to be a great thinker. Encourage him to always make sense. Tell him not to make things up and not to believe in magic. Teach him about cause and effect. Encourage him to live a life dedicated to reality and rational thinking.

# ADOLESCENCE

Adolescence is the most important stage of human development. It is a period of transition from childhood to adulthood. Your child's brain will experience significant development during adolescence. He will become more idealistic and more philosophical. He will also become more critical and more oppositional. Your adolescent may display angry outbursts now and then. He is trying to sort his life out and find a way to grow up. He does not hate you. If your child can harness his new ability for abstract and rational thought, he will be well able to mature and take on adult responsibility. Your child will have to learn to delay gratification and learn to self-regulate. Adolescence is a time of storm and stress regarding matters such as identity, body changes, sexuality, core beliefs, social relationships, and career choice. As a parent, be available to your adolescent. Keep the relationship warm, light, and easy. Communicate and negotiate with your adolescent. Encourage him to think for himself and to develop many essential life skills. Unhealthy adolescent rebellion may involve the use of drugs, opposition towards law enforcement, parental rejection, and dropping out of school. Healthy adolescent rebellion may include standing up to injustice, opposing racism, rejecting abusive parents, and formulating wholesome personal beliefs and values.

# PEACE WITH YOUR PAST

As a parent, you need to make peace with your past. Take responsibility where you must and acknowledge any victimization that you might have endured. Learn all that you can about yourself and examine all the factors that shaped your life. Carefully consider the impact of your family of orientation. Most people do the best that they can. Forgive yourself and forgive others. Maybe you were simply ignorant. Review the many times you were wronged. Train your mind to dwell on the many good people you have encountered and on the good memories. You may wish to tell your story to someone you trust. At some point you must surrender to the past and arrive at a place of calm acceptance. You cannot change the past. There is a long road ahead and it is a long game. Who told you that life was easy? Evaluate the impact of trauma on your life. Make peace with your past. Be whole and be healthy. Be the best parent that you can be.

# BODY HEALTH/BODY JOY

J oy is a body thing! We are happy within our bodies. It is difficult to be happy when your brain is foggy. It is difficult to be happy when you are experiencing physical pain. Make every effort to be physically healthy and keep your body working right. Eat nutritious food. Whole food is better than processed food. Get sufficient sleep. Exercise daily and drink an adequate amount of pure, clean water. When you engage in physical activity you are lifting your depression and reducing your anxiety level. Joy is sensations and vibrations pulsating throughout your body. This is what we experience when we go on a hike, when we play sports, or when we receive a massage. Observe the play and laughter of children. See how happy they are within their bodies. Hug your child and let your child hug you. Teach your child to love his body for joy is a body thing.

# MYSTERY

Life is a great mystery. We have many beliefs but few provable scientific facts regarding origin and destiny. There is the mystery of good and there is the mystery of evil. There is the mystery of love and there is the mystery of hate. There is the mystery of attraction between two people. There is the mystery of healing. Tremendous mystery! Delight yourself in the mystery of your existence and teach your child to do the same. Be at home with it. Accept life as a great mystery. There is much that we do not know. We will never have all the answers. Be rational with your beliefs and resist the temptation to make things up. Seek out the scientific evidence. Never apply simple solutions to life's complex problems. Understand that you are surrounded by mystery. We are mysterious creatures living mysterious lives in a mysterious environment. Slowly introduce your child to the mystery of his existence.

# SUICIDE

G lobally, more people die from suicide than from homicide. Some people descend into the dark tunnel of depression and never find their way back. People with mental health problems and physical health problems are especially vulnerable. There are many risk factors. Some people do not value life as a precious gift. Some people are weak and unable to properly handle suffering. Some people lack the mental toughness and the resiliency to solve problems. Some people are rigid in their thinking. For them, life is all or nothing. For some, suicidal thinking is a habit. Some people become overwhelmed by their chronic pain and become irrational and out of control. Anger, impulsivity, and emotionality are risk factors. It is important to live a meaningful life full of joy, creativity and productivity. Look at the big picture. You are not alone. You are part of a larger reality that is beyond yourself. Feelings cannot be trusted. They come and go and they keep changing. Your life circumstances can change. Today you may not have all the resources, help, and answers, but with time you can figure out a way forward. For your child, home must be a sanctuary and parents must be available for support and rescue. Talking about suicide with someone will not increase the risk of suicide. If a person shares with you that he is experiencing suicidal thoughts, he should be referred for professional intervention. Life is a precious gift to be valued and treasured. Make sure that your child has easy access to you so that he is well able to share his thoughts and his feelings and receive the support that he needs. We should all strive to make a meaningful contribution to the world. Have a cause and know that you are loved. As much as possible, keep your life simple and therefore manageable. Live for the people you love. Live for the people who love you and for the people who need you. Today, you might be on the verge of suicide. Tomorrow, you may be in a positive frame of mind. The only thing that changed is your perception of reality. Your thoughts and your feelings cannot be fully trusted. Suicide is final. Never give up and never give in to this evil monster.

# PROBLEM SOLVING

The first step in the process of problem solving is to define the problem. This will take time and effort. You will have to dig deep. There are two realities. One is surface reality and the other is a deeper, hidden reality. You must go beyond the surface. You may have to go back into the painful past. When you are able to define the problem, you will experience a sense of relief, a sense of power, and a sense of confidence. This, in itself, is therapy. The second step in the process of problem solving is to list all the possible solutions to the problem. Engage in creative brainstorming. Consider cause and effect. You must eventually settle on the one best possible solution. You may have to try several solutions before you find the one that really works. Consider all risks and benefits of the solution that you have selected. Learn to approach problem solving with bravery, creativity, and rational thought. As a parent, teach your child to define and solve problems.

# CONFIDENCE

Research suggests that there may be a genetic component to confidence. Extroverted people are not necessarily more confident than introverts. Confidence has something to do with intelligence, good physical health, and the acquisition of essential life skills. Exercise also contributes to self-confidence. Competence is a prerequisite to confidence so be good at what you do. As a parent, train your child to be an independent, open-minded, and divergent thinker. Teach your child to be assertive but never aggressive. Activities such as public speaking and sports will enhance your child's confidence. Remind your child to learn from his past mistakes and from the mistakes of others. Encourage him to move with rhythm and energy in the environment. A confident person is pleased with his success and is happy for the success of others. The opposite of confidence is weakness, dependency, and helplessness. As a parent, inspire your child through your confidence.

# ALWAYS RIGHT

Do not fight so hard to be right. There is much that we do not know. In the absence of facts, we have beliefs and beliefs are plentiful. Anyone can believe anything. Cultivate a spirit of openness, awareness, and a desire to learn. Do not be inflexible, or intolerant. You don't have all the correct answers. Some people rigidly cling to their early indoctrination. They are convinced that their beliefs are superior and more correct than the beliefs of others. Seek to learn and seek to understand others. Be a good listener. You are not always right. Do not be rigid and controlling. Value the other person's input. They may be more correct than you are. Give up the need to always be right and encourage your child to do the same.

# STRENGTHS AND WEAKNESSES

F ocus on your strengths and not on your weaknesses. Work with someone you trust to help you identify your strengths. Be aware of your weaknesses and work to improve them. Try to further refine and improve your strengths, for it will be your strengths that will lead you forward towards success. Some people have strong minds and tremendous inner strength. Some people are unselfish and considerate. Some people are natural actors, artists, and scientists. Some people are adept at mechanical tasks. Some people possess tremendous aptitude for technology. Some people are strong visual learners. Some people are blessed with ability for speech articulation and language comprehension. Some people possess fabulous ability for motor coordination and motor speed. Know your strengths. If your strength is visual learning, note cards and computers will be good tools for you to use in the learning process. As a parent, help your child to discover his strengths and encourage him to use his strengths to succeed.

# INDIVIDUALIZED APPROACHES

In the real world, averages are supremely important. They are representations of what is typical and within the range of normal. Averages are often determined through extensive research and mathematical calculations. Averages are important guidelines from which deviations from normal are calculated. As important as averages are, they are only guidelines. Your child is not a statistic. Your child is not a number. When instructing a child, parents and teachers should employ an individualized approach. Take into account the child's unique needs, his unique functioning, and the unique methods by which he learns. An individualized approach will pay huge dividends. As a parent, strive to individualize your approach to your child for he is a unique and special person.

# SOCIAL RELATIONSHIPS

Humans are social creatures. As a specie, we do not do well when we are socially isolated. Humans benefit greatly from meaningful social relationships with others. Maintaining any social relationship is challenging. People are different. People come from different cultures and backgrounds. We are the product of our indoctrination, our belief system, and our past experiences which may include emotional trauma. People possess different values, different temperaments, and different needs. Some people are not open minded and welcoming. Some people are rigid, dogmatic, and controlling. It is important to establish social relationships with people with whom you are compatible. At the same time, be mature enough to accept the differences in people and mature enough to appreciate their likes and dislikes. In every social relationship you have choices. You can choose to conflict or you can choose to compromise and keep the peace. It is important to cultivate a high regard for privacy and for social boundaries. It is also important to treat everyone with kindness, respect, and consideration. As a parent, encourage your child to develop social relationships with family members and friends who are kind, open-minded, and tolerant.

# A SIMPLE LIFE

S ome people live complicated lives. Many people overschedule themselves. Some people accumulate heaps of clutter. Some people have difficulty saying, "No". Many people are not able to separate their needs from their wants. Some people are driven by high anxiety or the need to compete. Some are people pleasers who are overly concerned about the opinions of others. Some people are poor planners who live a disorganized and chaotic life. The messages that we receive through television and print encourage us to purchase things that we do not need. We often desire to have the things that other people possess. Some people live beyond their means. Some people constantly compare themselves to others. Slow down. Get rid of the clutter. Practice gratitude for what you have and learn to live a simple and manageable life. Enjoy the simple things in life such as planting a garden, walking in nature, and fixing a simple meal. Life can become quite complicated. If you keep it simple, your life will be less stressful. Simplicity will enhance your physical and mental health. As a parent, teach your child to live a simple life.

# WISDOM

With knowledge comes understanding. With knowledge, understanding, and experience comes wisdom. With an open mind, analyze every experience so that you can learn a useful lesson. Be a thinking person. A great part of our wisdom comes from meaningful life experiences and on-the-job training. Wisdom demands that we seek to understand ourselves first before we attempt to understand others. Do not be in a hurry to judge. Behaviors are explainable. Walk in a person's shoes. Feel their pain and feel their joy. Observe well and communicate clearly. Read a person's body language, including facial expressions and tone of voice. Spend time with great thinkers who are open-minded. Read books on a variety of challenging subjects. Remember, there is a lot that we do not know. Cultivate a willingness to change your beliefs when you are confronted with scientific evidence and rational ideas. Develop your intuition and your ability for sound judgement. Wisdom demands that you analyze your mistakes and learn from them. Wisdom demands that you analyze the mistakes of others and learn from them. Wisdom demands that you never repeat your mistakes. As a parent, help your child to grow in knowledge, understanding, and wisdom.

# SUCCESS

The word success means different things to different people. The definition of success depends on a person's beliefs and values. Some people view success as achieving a solid education. Some people define success in terms of the accumulation of wealth. Some people feel successful when they are able to make creative and useful contributions that improve society. There should always be a positive and wholesome aspect to your definition of success. A bank robber may consider robbing banks without getting caught as a success. Others will view his self-defeating behavior as utter failure. In life, it is important to know what is for you and what is not for you. We are all different. Do not compete with others. Do not compare your life with others. It will always be a false comparison. Life is about limited time. Invest in your health. Create joyful memories. Contribute something tangible to planet earth. Lend a helping hand. Remain on the side of goodness and truth. Do the best that you can. At the end of the journey, be able to look back with pride on the life you have lived and the contributions you have made.

# ADDICTIONS

Humans form habits easily – good or bad. Behavior that is reinforced by a pay-off is often repeated. A pay-off can come from within such as a good feeling, or originate from the outside such as parental praise or a monetary reward. There are healthy addictions and there are unhealthy addictions. Some healthy addictions are exercise, positive social interactions, and sports. Some unhealthy addictions are smoking, eating junk food, and gambling. Help your child to develop healthy addictions such as exercise, music, and gardening. We can become excessive with a healthy addiction so cultivate a balanced approach. By teaching and by example, help your child to become addicted to kindness and goodness. Allow him to experience the good feeling that comes with making others happy. Help him to become addicted to the idea of making the world a better place. Any good behavior that you practice will soon become a healthy addiction and a wonderful habit.

# SELF-EVALUATION

Your child does not possess the brain power or life experience to properly evaluate his own functioning. He is not capable of abstract thought, or philosophical thinking. The adults in his life, especially his parents and teachers, should take it upon themselves to provide feedback to him regarding his overall functioning. Your child may not be fully aware of himself as he moves about in his environment. Sometimes a video works quite well. Give your child feedback in an indirect and non-threatening manner without any judgement. Some areas of focus are physical functioning, thinking skills, and social behaviors. Parents should also engage in self-evaluation. Be aware of the impact that you are having on your child. You may wish to solicit feedback from someone you trust. As a parent, teach your child that self-evaluation is a prerequisite for self-regulation.

# REPRESSION

As humans, we have a tendency to bury painful and uncomfortable emotions in the deeper layers of our mind well out of the reach of our awareness. These negative feelings are often produced by traumatic experiences. These repressed feelings can fester and ferment at a deep level causing us to be sad, angry, anxious, or fearful. If, as a child, you were chased and bitten by a dog, you may have grown up with a repressed fear of dogs, or maybe a fear of animals in general. Remaining emotionally repressed is not a good thing. Encourage your child to express his feelings using his words. Give him an opportunity to tell his story. As a parent, one of your toughest jobs is to protect your child from experiencing trauma. You will only succeed some of the time. Create many positive experiences, and therefore great memories, for your child. Good memories will serve to counteract the bad experiences.

# REGRESSION

M any people regress when life becomes difficult. Some adults may become dependent and babyish when they are physically sick. Many children will slip back to an earlier and more comfortable level of development when they experience trauma or when they face challenges. Your child may regress upon the arrival of a new sibling. As a parent, it is important to spend special time with your child doing fun activities. The goal in life is to move forward. The child most likely to regress is the one who is lacking in age-appropriate essential life skills, for it is skills that give us confidence to take on challenging and difficult tasks. Some children function with high anxiety. Some children may be weak and dependent. If your child displays regressive behaviors, help him to start moving forward again. Encourage him to complete a few age-appropriate tasks. Praise him for his accomplishments. As a parent, your job is to provide a safe, loving, and secure environment for your child. Do not get angry with your child when he regresses. Encourage him to do the things he can do for himself. Always be encouraging, supportive, and reassuring. Parenting involves a great deal of coaching. Teach your child to problem solve. Remind him of his areas of strength. Praise his every success so that he will grow in confidence. Listen to your child and provide many opportunities for him to express himself through daily conversations. Get your child outdoors for some exercise. Teach him to relax and enjoy some quiet time. Make sure that he is physically healthy and is sleeping well. Make his life predictable by following a daily schedule. Teach him to use silent inner language to calm himself. The more essential life skills your child possesses, the more confident he will become.

# PLAY

Play is fun and play is essential to your child's well-being. Play with your baby from the beginning. Your child will feel loved and valued. Teach your older child to get his work done before play. Through play, your child will learn team-work, social skills, and conflict resolution. Playtime affords opportunities for self-expression and creativity. Play activities will contribute to the refinement of his motor skills and the development of his imagination and thinking ability. Through play your child will develop his communication skills and reduce his stress. Structured play will teach your child about following rules and directions. Structured play may involve the development of specific skills. Unstructured play is self-chosen. Through unstructured play, your child will develop his own ideas and his creativity. Unstructured play will also provide opportunities for decision making and independent thinking. Play is a fun way to establish a healthy balance to one's life. Children and adults should play every day. Structured and unstructured play will bring your child great joy and contribute greatly to his physical and mental health.

# A LARGE WORLD VIEW

Help your child to cultivate a large world view. Be a good example for your child. Look at the big picture. Strive to develop true and realistic beliefs about the world. Be careful with labels. Be careful with oversimplified generalizations about people based on gender, race, culture, religion, and sexual orientation. Cultivate an open mind that is filled with tolerance, kindness, and compassion. Learn all that you can from other cultures and other religions. Spend time with people who are different. Humans have a great deal in common. Be accepting of and be fascinated by cultural differences. Never throw groups of people in the same basket. Learn to look at issues from a personal, national, and global point of view. Seek to understand others and be a big picture person. Help to give your child a large world view.

# FORGIVENESS

No one is perfect. Forgive yourself. You are only human. Forgive others. They are only human. Forgiveness is more about you than about them. Let it go so that you can be at peace. Let go of your anger. Forgive so that you can heal. When you forgive, the offender has no more power over you. Offer up the hurt to the love and to the goodness that is within you. Forgive so that you do not remain wounded. Forgive and move on. Forgiveness is important to your mental health. Teach your child to forgive.

# TAKE SOME TIME TO
# WASTE SOME TIME

The things we see, the things we hear, and all the things that we do will drain us physically and mentally. Learn to relax and waste some time. Take some time to have some fun. We do not need to be productive all day long. Do not over-schedule yourself. Try not to take life too seriously. Sometimes you win and sometimes you lose. Play with friends. Learn to laugh and have fun. Play and relaxation are therapeutic and essential to your physical and mental health. Take time to waste time. Slow down. Death is your final destination. Why be in a hurry? As a parent, make sure your child gets an opportunity to play every day.

# GOOD MEMORIES

L ife is about limited time and the accumulation of memories. Help your child to create good memories every day. These good memories will serve as cushions when tough times come. Good memories give us hope for the future. They remind us that good times will come again. Let your child see new places. Take pictures. A warm and loving interaction with a friend or relative can be a great memory. Engage in simple activities such as playing catch, enjoying a cookout, or going for a hike in nature. Encourage your child to perform daily acts of kindness. Good deeds are great memories. Good memories are one of the greatest gifts you can give to your child.

# BULLYING

Bullying is unwanted aggressive behaviors towards another that are intended to humiliate or intimidate. In some cases, there is a difference in the balance of power. As a parent, do not bully your child. Do not yell at your child and do not threaten or hit your child. Excessive control, criticism, and name calling are bullying. Be on the alert for indications that your child is being bullied at school or in the community. A child that is being bullied may show injuries. He may return home without some of his possessions. He may become fearful of going to school or fearful of going outside to play. A child that is bullied may become angry, depressed, or suicidal. His school grades may decline. If you suspect that your child is being bullied at school, do not hesitate to ask for a child study meeting to discuss the matter. Your child's teacher and the school principal should be in attendance. As a parent, you may ask that the school bully stay at least ten feet away from your child. Let your child know that he can come to you if he is being bullied at school or in the neighborhood. He may be fearful that bullying will get worse if he reports it. Reassure him that reporting bullying is the right thing to do and that you can help. An introverted child may become the target of bullying. On the other hand, your angry and aggressive child may be a bully. Know his friends. Are they kind and caring? As a parent, listen carefully to what your child says about others. If you suspect that your child is a bully, you must seek professional help for him. As a parent, be aware of cyberbullying through social media. Bullying is destructive. All humans are sacred and should be approached with reverence and care.

# BECOMING A GOOD STUDENT

G uide your child into becoming a good student. Make sure your child is physically healthy. Balanced nutrition and quality sleep are supremely important. Teach your child to be compliant. Teach your child to sit still and complete a simple task. Train your child to become an independent worker by encouraging him and by only providing help when help is needed. Instill in your child a love for learning. Let your child see you read and do research. Have daily conversations with him. Cultivate your child's curiosity by pointing out details in the natural world. When your child is eager to learn, he is quite teachable. Help your child to live a structured life by following a schedule for work, play, and sleep. Train your child to manage his time in an efficient manner. Help your child to develop strong abstract vocabulary and strong visual recall. As your child gets older, help him to be organized with his homework and with his note taking. Provide a quiet place for your child to study that is away from television and the phone.

# TOXIC PARENTS

T oxic parents exhibit a range of negative behaviors that may cause emotional damage to a child. Some toxic parents are self-centered, unloving, and manipulative. Some toxic parents are rigid and controlling, even angry and violent. Some toxic parents are "do nothing" parents who are simply permissive. They may yell at their child and threaten them without applying any consequences. Some toxic parents are driven by irrational fears and phobias. Some toxic parents are emotionally dead and some are not grounded in reality. Some toxic parents are not able to have a warm and healthy conversation with their child. Some toxic parents are unable to get down to a child's level and play with them in a joyful and loving manner. Some toxic parents have little regard for privacy and boundaries. They overexpose their child to adult concerns and seek to use their child to meet their own emotional needs. As a parent, be aware of your own functioning and of the impact you are having on your child. Stop the negative behaviors before it all ends in disaster. If you are out of control, you should seek professional help.

# YOUR FRIGHTENED CHILD

As soon as your child becomes aware of the dangers that are in the world, he will become frightened. One of your main goals, as a parent, is to protect your child from trauma and give him a sense of safety. Find ways to lower your child's stress level. Help him to develop a range of essential life skills so that he can feel both competent and confident. Trauma can result from events such as storms, death, and crime. Trauma can also be subtle as in the case of witnessing horror or believing that something terrible took place. From birth get a soft quilt for your child to lie on for quiet time. Hug your child to provide contact comfort. Although the world is a dangerous place, most of the things that we worry about never happen. Be realistic, cautious, and preventive in your approach. As your child grows up you must present to him a balanced view of the world. There is beauty and there is danger in the world. There are good people and there are evil people. The goal is to gravitate towards the good while trying to escape the evil. Your child will struggle to understand and accept the concept of death. Encourage your child to express himself and to ask questions. Let him know that there are many things that we do not know. As a parent, bring your own anxieties under control and do not engage in irrational thinking and irrational behaviors. Routines will add predictability to your child's life and serve to reduce his stress. Give him frequent backrubs. Take his input seriously so that he can feel effective and confident.

Your child will become frightened if you are frightened. Comfort him. Some events in life are serious and some events are minor difficulties. Help him to know the difference. Do not over-react. Encourage your child to express his fears. He must learn to face the future with bravery. He must learn to take well-calculated risks. He must not be controlled by his fears. Teach him to use emotional words such as sad, angry, and scared. Daily exercise, conversations, sports, and gardening are wholesome activities that will reduce his stress. A frightened child who acquires a range of essential life skills will have the confidence to grow up and become independent.

# BEHAVIOR MANAGEMENT

As a parent, be loving yet firm. Teach your child to comply promptly to your request. Get rid of the irrational fear that your child will not love you if you discipline him. The goals of behavior management are to first keep your child safe in the world, and then to teach him how to behave in socially appropriate ways. Be consistent with the consequences that you apply to his behaviors. Do not spank your child. Instead, talk to your child and reason with him. Hitting your child's body is risky. It models aggression and you are risking injury to your child. Spanking a child devalues him. When you hit your child, he will feel that he has instantly paid the price for his misbehavior. He does not have to sit and feel bad for his inappropriate behaviors. Spanking a child will therefore interfere with the development of his conscience. Be a good example for your child. The one best thing that you can do for your child is to praise his good behaviors. Say, "Thank you for being good". Teach your child to know the difference between right and wrong. Behaviors are right when they help others and make them happy. Behaviors are wrong when they hurt others and make them feel sad. Speaking with a soft but firm voice say, "Please do this now". Do not get into the habit of paying money to your child for the completion of his schoolwork, for doing his household chores, or for his good behaviors. You may choose to surprise him with a reward now and then for just being good. When your child misbehaves, you should apply a negative consequence to his misconduct such as a time out. For an older child do not hesitate to say, "That was bad behavior – shame on that behavior". You are shaming the poor behavior. You are not shaming your child. A measure of shame and guilt for bad behaviors will help him to develop his conscience. Chronic misbehavior in your child may be a sign that he is stressed, bullied, or simply not sleeping well. As a parent, create many good experiences for your child. Teach him that being a good person is the easiest and most rewarding way to live in the world. Help him to develop a tremendous capacity to love.

# SEXUAL UNFOLDING

Some people are uncomfortable talking about human sexuality. Do not be one of them. Your child is a sexual creature. Human sexuality is as normal and natural as being right-handed. Remember the important goals: to raise a child that is a wonderful blend of male and female qualities, to help your child learn appropriate sexual conduct, to help your child establish and follow well-defined personal boundaries, and to place sexuality within the context of love and respect. Ignore your child's touching of his or her genitals. Ignore your young son's spontaneous erections. Relax. Both are innocent and normal. Remind your child that self-pleasuring is a private behavior. Be a good example of love and intimacy. Let your child see you hug and kiss. As a parent, be affectionate with your child. These simple experiences will benefit him greatly when he becomes an adult. If, through curiosity, your child engages in the showing or touching of his private body parts, do not panic. Let him know that private parts are not for showing. Teach him about private behaviors. You do not want your child to associate guilt with sexuality. Always use the proper names for body parts. When your child asks questions, give him the shortest, simplest, and most honest answer that is appropriate for his age.

# DAILY CONVERSATIONS

Have one-way conversations with your baby before he is born. Have one-way conversations with your baby after he is born. Your child will love the interaction and he will respond to your voice, smile, and facial expressions. Have daily conversations with your child that are meaningful and positive. Share trivia that is realistic and sensible. Daily conversations will strengthen the bond between you and your child. In addition, his language and thinking skills will be enhanced. Through daily conversations, your child will have an opportunity to express his thoughts and his feelings. For the child who does not like to read, daily conversations will help him acquire knowledge. Ask your child questions and challenge his thinking. Develop realistic scenarios about real life situations and have your child brainstorm with you. Daily conversations may include some story telling regarding your own childhood. There are lessons to be learned. Daily conversations will help your child to develop confidence. As you talk to your child, remind him to slow down and relax. Schools should consider hiring bright, loving teachers whose sole responsibility is to have daily, wholesome, stimulating conversations with students. It is a form of therapy.

# EMOTIONAL DEVELOPMENT

Your child's emotional development is as important as his physical, social, or intellectual development. Provide a sense of safety and comfort for your child. As a parent, build trust by keeping your word and by sharing trivial information with your child. Hug your child many times every day. When he is frightened, hold him so that he can feel safe. When he is tired, soothe and comfort him. Always praise your child for his efforts and for his successes. Tell your child wonderful stories about your childhood. Tell your child about his birth circumstances and how special he is. Allow your child to make mistakes and to learn from his mistakes. Always call your child by his name for his name is special. Encourage your child to express himself. Always reassure your child that he is loved and tell him often that you are proud of him. Expose your child to the beauty of nature. Have him care for little plants. A cuddly toy is good for your child. Allow your child to play with mud and water. Let him experience texture and engage in creativity and calmness. Teach your child to be kind through your example of kindness. Laugh out loud with your child. Home should be a happy and relaxed place. Teach your child to manage his emotions, especially his anger. Coach him into naming and expressing his feelings. Share your feelings with him. Be warm and loving but do not cultivate dependency. Let your child do things for himself with your guidance and with your assistance. Help your child to develop a tremendous capacity to love.

# THE JOYS OF LAUGHTER

Be deliberate in bringing laughter into your home. Tell some jokes and laugh out loud. Give your child the gift of laughter. It will enhance his physical and mental health. Through laughter your child will become happy and confident. Watch some wholesome comedy movies with your child. Get rid of the rigidity. Loosen up and laugh a little. Do not be a punitive parent. Do not yell at your child and do not threaten your child. Do not add to the pain that is already in the world. Laughter will boost your child's immune system and help to give him a more positive attitude towards life. Laughter will reduce his stress. Humans are highly hilarious creatures. Laugh at yourself and laugh at situations that are funny. Reduce the tension in your life. Laughter is fun and laughter is free. Laughter is great therapy.

# SACREDNESS AND REVERENCE

Your child is a sacred being. Always approach him with reverence. Be patient, loving, and understanding. Never hurt your child. Never be rough with your baby and never shake him. If you regard all human life as sacred, you will never hate or discriminate. Sacredness and reverence will become the guiding principle by which you live your life. People in positions of power who live by this philosophy will treat others with sensitivity and with kindness. The weak, the poor, and the defenseless will be protected. Sacredness is about value and reverence is about treating people with care regardless of their age, gender, race, sexual orientation, or beliefs.

# ABSTRACT ABILITY

M any children experience difficulty in school because they lack abstract ability. You can help your child develop good language comprehension skills by helping him to understand the meaning of abstract words. Do not depend on your school to do this. If you have a table, you can see the table and you can touch the table. This is concrete learning. Abstract learning involves concepts such as above the table and below the table. Demonstrate and explain abstract concepts to your child. You may obtain a list of abstract words from your child's teacher. Some other examples of abstract words are slow, fast, full, empty, sad, and happy. Encourage your child to hold an abstract concept in his mind for a period of time. Ask him to think about it. Have him picture abstract concepts in his mind such as slow walking and fast walking. Show your child pictures that demonstrate an abstract concept such as full and empty. Show your child a glass of water that is full. Throw half of the water away and show your child what half-empty means. Then, throw away all the water and teach your child the meaning of the word empty. Exercises in abstract thinking will raise your child's intelligence and enhance his learning ability.

# ASKING FOR HELP

Some people find it difficult to ask for help. Some people are simply private and some people are non-trusting. Some people view asking for help as a sign of weakness. There is plenty of free assistance that is available in your community. Your school's social worker can be helpful. If you are a new mother, seek the help of a mature and nurturing friend or relative. As a parent, if you are experiencing significant depression, you must seek professional help. Experiencing depression does not mean that you are a bad or incompetent parent. Reach out to your child's pediatrician right away if you have urges to hurt your baby. Taking care of a child is stressful. Have a trusted friend or relative help care for your baby so that you can have a break to rest and relax. Unfortunately, society has stigmatized mental health problems and sometimes people become ashamed of their mental health issues. Do not be one of them. Seek the help that you need. Mental health problems do not simply cure themselves.

# LIKE A SPONGE

Your child is like a sponge. He will soak up everything that you say and everything that you do. Children are sensitive creatures. They learn a lot by imitation. Your child will soak up your attitude, your moods, your likes, and your dislikes. Your child will think like you, speak like you, and act like you. If you are organized, responsible, and effective, your child will soak that up. If you possess a large world view and an open heart, your child will soak that up. Your child will soak up what you value, and how you treat people. If you are rigid, anxious, reckless, and violent, your child will soak that up. If you are serene, peaceful, confident, and strong, your child will soak that up. If you are bigoted and racist, your child will soak that up. Provide positive and wholesome experiences for your child. One day your child will develop the brain power to analyze the impact you had on him. Be careful. Your child is like a sponge.

# SENSORY STIMULATION

Your child's development will be enhanced by the stimulation of his five senses – touch, sight, hearing, smell, and taste. Touch your child softly and frequently as you call his name. This is a way of providing stimulation and comfort at the same time. Give your child experience with a variety of textures – hard, soft, rough, smooth, and slippery. Do not tickle or shake your baby. Let your young child play with water and mud. With supervision, an older child can experience the feel of water that is gently sprayed from a garden hose. Allow your child to touch a variety of foods with his hand. Your baby's room should be colorful. As he grows older, teach him to look at large pictures. Take your child outdoors so that he can see a variety of objects. A trip to the zoo will be quite stimulating. Introduce large puzzles and movies to your older child. Talk to your baby before he is born. Read to your baby before he is born. To stimulate your child's hearing, you can bang softly on objects that make different sounds. Talk to your child. Play a variety of music to him. Read to your child and have conversations with him. Let him experience different sounds coming from different locations in the house. If your child is noise sensitive, you will have to lower the volume of the sound. Expose your child to a variety of smells including flowers, herbs, and foods. You can keep your child close to the kitchen so that he can experience the aroma of your cooking and your baking. When it comes to different tastes, go slowly. Introduce sweet and sour foods to your child. Stimulate and integrate your child's sensory abilities through everyday experiences.

# NUTRITION FOR YOUR CHILD

Nutritious food is important for your child's overall health and performance. Children consume a great deal of energy through the use of their brains and through physical activity such as playing. Make good choices and begin to develop healthy eating habits in your child from the beginning. Work with your pediatrician to develop a personalized nutrition program for your infant. There are good foods and there are bad foods. Prepare balanced meals at home with adequate amounts of protein, healthy fats, and whole food carbohydrates. Processed, packaged, and canned foods are to be avoided as much as possible. Increase the consumption of fresh fruits and vegetables. Cooked cereal may be healthier than boxed cereal. Whole grain bread may be better than white bread. Use olive oil instead of vegetable oil. As much as possible avoid foods grown with the use of pesticides, herbicides, or antibiotics. Sugar and salt should be used in moderation. Have your child drink pure water instead of soft drinks. You may wish to dilute fruit juices or better still have your child eat the whole fruit. Junk food should be avoided. Provide fruits and vegetables as snacks. There are recipes available on the internet for healthy home-made nutrition bars. Your child will develop healthy eating habits if you consistently provide healthy foods for him. Physical activity and mental work will drain your child's energy. Nutritious food will help to fuel your child's body throughout the day.

# YOUR GIFTED CHILD

Your child may be gifted. Very often, it is a classroom teacher who is the first to spot giftedness in children. These students are often early readers who excel at academic tasks. They often have a great command of language and display strengths with logical reasoning and abstract ability. Gifted children may exhibit a wide range of interests. Often, they are independent workers who are sensitive and curious. At home and at school gifted children may ask a lot of questions and in general they talk a great deal. Gifted children learn fast and many of them are easily bored and somewhat oppositional. When a school-age child is suspected of being gifted, he is evaluated for intelligence, academic skills, and gifted characteristics. Like all children, a gifted child should be taught in an individualized manner with emphasis on his strengths and interests. Do not encourage early specialization. Let your gifted child live a relaxed and balanced life. Help him develop his social skills and allow many opportunities for self-expression. Encourage your gifted child to participate in art, music, sports, and writing. Teach him to follow a daily schedule. Make him responsible for household chores. Remind your gifted child that he is a child and not an adult. Engage your gifted child in daily conversations and encourage him to cultivate a large world view filled with love, flexibility, respect, and tolerance for all people. Do not overschedule your gifted child and do not push him into activities that he dislikes. Teach your gifted child to help those who are less capable. Let your gifted child know that he is blessed with talent but do not pressure him.

# HOMEWORK

Gifted children learn quickly and they learn a great deal on their own. Many of them require little or no teaching. Intellectually gifted children do not need homework. On the other hand, slow learners need a great deal of instruction and practice. They may benefit from a small amount of homework that is well planned. Slow learners will likely need the help of parents to complete their homework. Unfortunately, assigned homework will cut into family time and into your child's play time. Homework is often a source of conflict between a child and his parent. In place of homework, a parent may wish to involve their child in the learning process through reading, conversations, and educational videos. There are no research findings to suggest that the tradition of homework is beneficial for anyone. One suggestion is that teachers help their students to complete their academic tasks at school where they can receive assistance and guidance from the classroom teacher. By so doing, there will be less stress on the family regarding homework. If your child's school has a policy that homework is for everyone, you as a parent will have to negotiate the volume of your child's homework with the classroom teacher.

# PRACTICE-PRACTICE-PRACTICE

We become whatever we practice. If you practice running you will become a good runner. If you practice kindness, you will become a kind person. If you practice peacefulness, you will become a peaceful person. Your child will become a good reader if he practices his reading. Your child's brain will remember whatever he practices. Humans form habits easily through repeated practice. If your child practices impulse control by stopping himself, he will be well able to control himself. Your child will improve his thinking skills by the practice of brainstorming solutions to problems. Your child will develop rhythm by listening to music, by dancing, and by beating on a drum pad. As a parent, it is your responsibility to schedule time for your child to physically practice academic skills, physical skills, and social skills. Your child can also engage in effective mental practice through the process of visualization. Your child will become skilled at whatever he practices.

# GRADE RETENTION

As a parent, never agree to grade retention. There is no evidence that holding your child back for another year in the same grade is a positive experience. The trauma of grade retention will affect your child negatively for the rest of his life. Some children who are retained may become angry and depressed. They may feel ashamed and they may feel like a failure. Children who are retained may develop a damaged sense of self as they see their friends promoted to the next grade. The teacher and the school principal may try to convince you that grade retention will allow time for your child to develop readiness skills and maturity. The trauma of grade retention is too great. Giving your child another year of the same program makes no sense. In regards to academic failure, the focus always seems to be on the child and his deficits and not on the deficits in the teacher and the school system. Struggling children will benefit more from individualized and strategic instruction than from grade retention. If your child is receiving exceptional education, there is no reason why he should be retained. If your child is struggling in regular education, his case should be discussed by the child study team comprised of his parents, the school principal, his classroom teacher, the school psychologist, the school social worker, and the school nurse. The child's problem should be clearly defined and specific interventions should be prescribed. Progress should be carefully monitored. Some children are visual learners who experience language comprehension difficulty. The school psychologist should help the classroom teacher to design a program for the child with learning problems that emphasizes visual learning. The child study team should discuss the possible role of stress and poor sleep on the child's academic underachievement. Grade retention is a bad idea that can lead to school dropout.

# YOUR CHILD'S AUTHENTIC SELF

Your child is a special person. If you observe him closely and if you listen to him carefully, you will discover his uniqueness and his special qualities. Never let your child lose his authentic self. Your child may be outgoing or he may be reserved. Help him to accept his authentic self. Your child may be musical with a good sense of rhythm. Your child may be a quiet thinker with great ideas and outstanding problem-solving skills. Some children are mechanically inclined. Work with your child to identify and develop his strengths. Some children are highly externalized and will readily engage with the outside world. Some children are highly internalized with a rich inner life. Coach and guide your child but at the same time help him to retain his authentic self. Your job is to help your child find his path and become a fully functioning adult who is independent from you. Help your child on his way to self-discovery. Accept your child for the person he is, and your child will learn to accept himself. He will take great pride in being real and authentic.

# DIVORCE AND YOUR CHILD

The high rate of divorce is a direct reflection on the challenges of marriage. When divorce happens, your major goal as a parent is to minimize the trauma to your child. Divorce should be viewed as a functional arrangement that society uses to bring abusive marriages to an end. Let your child know well in advance if there is going to be a separation. Children regard their parents as omnipotent. Divorce will shatter this belief and trigger feelings of despair, anger, and confusion. In the event of a divorce, it will be important to reassure your child that he is not to blame. Divorce is between the parents. Your child may experience separation anxiety and functional regression. Help your child to feel safe and secure. In the interest of your child, parents should always be respectful and supportive of each other. Your child may experience a range of problems including sleep difficulty, behavior disorder, and a drop in school grades. At some point in time, you may wish to apologize to your child for the trauma of divorce. Your child will need reassurance and rescue.

# CHILD ABUSE AND NEGLECT

The physical, emotional, or sexual abuse of a child is a horrific crime. In a preventive sense, rights, privacy, and boundaries within a household must be well respected. Children should learn to sleep in their own beds. Child neglect is about failure to supervise your child and failure to provide a safe environment for him. Child neglect also includes failure to provide adequate food, clothing, or shelter for your child. Never shake your baby. There is no reason to beat your child. Teach him to be compliant. Apply rules and consequences in a consistent manner. Demonstrate proper behaviors to your child so that he can learn. Praise his good behaviors. Train your child to be socially appropriate. Parenting is about teaching, coaching, and the modeling of good conduct. The emotional abuse of a child is quite subtle. Yelling at your child is abusive. Embarrassing your child is abusive. Laughing at your child's failure is abusive. Willfully putting your child in a frightening situation is abusive. It is abusive when you place demands on your child that he clearly cannot fulfill. Rejection of your child is abusive. You are being abusive when you overcriticize your child. When you recall your child's failure and shame him you are being abusive. When you display anger and loss of control in front of your child, you are being abusive. You are being emotionally abusive when you criticize and undermine your child's classroom teacher. Exposing your child to adult topics and adult materials is abusive. As a parent, always be loving and kind to your child.

# STORIES AND POEMS

Read stories and poems to your child before he is born. Let your child experience the sweetness of your voice. Read stories about the lives of good people. Read books about love and goodness. Read stories that will encourage your child to imagine and pretend. Read sweet poems to your child. Books of children's poetry are available. Make reading a daily activity in your home. Read material that is positive and full of hope. Read about people solving problems and making good things happen. Teach your child to read. You can then buy him books of animal stories to enjoy. Have conversations about the stories that your child is reading. Reading stories and poems to your child is a way to build his intellectual ability, strengthen his attachment to you, and create fond memories. Tell stories to your child. Tell about the adventures of your own childhood. Cuddle your child while you are telling him stories and while you are reading poems to him. What a great memory!

# KINDNESS AND SHARING

Teach your child to be kind. Be a good example by doing kind deeds for others. Teach your child to be kind to plants and to animals. Train him to be kind and gentle in all of his interactions. It is a good way to live. When you perform kind deeds, everyone is blessed – the giver of kindness, the receiver of kindness, and the observer of kindness. The giver of kindness will be happy and fulfilled. The receiver of kindness will be overjoyed, thankful, and less frightened living in the world. The observer of kindness will walk away thrilled and filled with hope upon witnessing people taking care of each other. Kindness is therefore a form of therapy. When you teach kindness to your child, you are helping him to develop conscience. People with conscience will not knowingly hurt others. If you deliberately perform acts of kindness for others, you will soon become a kind person. Teach your child to share. Be a good example of sharing what you have with others. One act of kindness and sharing can become a wonderful and lasting memory for your child.

# TRUTH AND HONESTY

There are some absolute truths. The earth is round. Two plus two is four. Humans are born and humans die. You cannot walk on water. If you jump out of a ten-story building you will fall to the ground. There are different levels of truth. Some people regard their personal beliefs as their personal truth as opposed to scientific truth. Verifiable truth is often backed up by scientific evidence and in many cases can be replicated under controlled conditions. Emotional truth is personal and has to do with what you are feeling. Objective truth is often backed up by science. Subjective truth may be personal beliefs and opinions. There are many flavors of truth. Perhaps the most important truth is truth to yourself. Always strive to cultivate personal truth that is wholesome, constructive, and kind. Never try to impose your personal truth on others. Be flexible instead of rigid. Be understanding, respectful, and tolerant of other people's truth. Another aspect to truth is honesty. Do not take advantage of another person. In all of your dealings, be fair and reasonable. Live out your wholesome truth and always be honest.

# TEACHING AND COACHING

As a parent, it is your job to teach your child. Do not depend on your school or your church to instruct your child. He must learn to live in the real world. He must understand how the real world works and what is required of him to survive in it. You teach by telling him and you teach by showing him. Praise your child for every success. Call his name and tell him that you are proud of him. There are essential life skills that he will need to learn such as sitting still, completing a task, and following a schedule. Help your child to further develop his strengths while you work to remediate his weaknesses. Help your child to develop strong visual memory by showing him pictures for later recall. Ask your child open-ended questions. You can build your child's ability to concentrate by having him listen to and repeat back a series of random numbers. As a parent, put the emphasis on incidental learning through conversations, projects, and field trips. The school is responsible for structured learning. Teach your child to be socially appropriate at all times. Have daily conversations with your child. Be a good coach. Break down the task you are teaching him into manageable steps and involve your child in repeated practice. Praise his success. Let your child learn by observing and by engaging in hands-on experience. Make sure the assigned task is within your child's ability range. Be patient. Skills will build his confidence and his effectiveness.

# LEARNING TO OBSERVE

We talk too much and we observe too little. Teach your child to observe. Take him out in nature and point out details in the natural world. We are highly visual creatures with tremendous ability for enjoyment and for learning. Be still and observe. Remind your child to always observe his environment and to be aware of danger. Teach him to observe people. Are they calm or aggressive? Look at their faces, especially their eyes. Watch their movements. As a parent, carefully observe your child. Children are not straightforward. They will not tell you much. You must learn to read your child the way you read a book. Read his general energy level, posture, and coping ability. Look for behavior changes. Is your child looking frightened, sad, or angry? Observe your child at play. Is he kind and sharing. Is he socially appropriate? Observe your child's language performance, especially his tone of voice, his articulation, and his command of language. Observe your child's ability to smile and relax. Is your child expressive, independent, and confident, or is he helpless, dependent, and rigid? As your child gets older, introduce the concept of self-awareness to him so that he can learn to self-evaluate and learn to self-regulate.

# THE BIRACIAL CHILD

There are millions of biracial children. Many of them grow up to be happy and successful. On the other hand, many biracial children struggle with identity. Many of them are bullied. Parents of a biracial child should strive to be respectful and supportive of each other. Both parents should encourage their biracial child to learn about both cultures and celebrate diversity. As parents, encourage your child to identify with both races. Society will label your child and there is no way around that. Your child is not a label. Help him to forge his own identity as a good person. Your biracial child did not choose his beginning. Help him to love himself and delight himself in his heritage. Every child is special. It will help if you live in a multiethnic neighborhood. It will also help if your biracial child is involved in extracurricular activities with other children of mixed backgrounds. As parents, form supportive friendships with other parents of biracial children. You cannot change society. You can only change yourself and make good choices. Parents and teachers should work together in the interest of the biracial child. Both parties should be on the alert for bullying. Encourage your biracial child to express himself and to share his concerns with his parents and with his teacher. Every child is precious.

# THE CHILD RAISED
# IN POVERTY

Poor children come from all racial groups. Many poor children are raised by single parents. Children raised in poverty often lack adequate food, clothing, and shelter. Many poor children live in dangerous neighborhoods plagued by gang activity and gun violence. Many poor children live a life of constant worry and stress. In general, poor children receive inadequate health care. They often attend the worst schools in the nation where resources are scarce. Many poor children live in unsafe homes and are exposed to toxic materials. Many poor children arrive at school hungry and lacking in readiness skills. Parents who live in poverty struggle to survive and often they fail to provide the care and stimulation that a child needs. If you are a parent living in poverty, reach out to community resources. The school social worker can be extremely helpful. Call your local church. Inquire about free clinics. Join the local library. As a parent, limit your child's time with television and video games. Read to your child every day and have him read to you. Train your child to sit still and complete a simple task. Have daily conversations with your child. Get him to bed on time. Make sure that your child has breakfast and make sure that he attends school every day. Take preventive measures that will keep your child safe. Purchase nutritious food for your child – protein, carbohydrates, fruits, and vegetables. Teach your child to know the difference between right and wrong. Train your child to be compliant and to be socially appropriate. Teach your child to control himself, to make good choices, and to respect the police. Make sure that you can fully trust the people with whom you leave your child. Work closely with your child's teacher. Remind your child often that a good education is his ticket out of poverty.

# THE MONSTER CALLED
# REPRESSED RAGE

Your child's mind may be full of repressed rage that is connected to an earlier emotional trauma. He may display physical symptoms such as body tension, headaches, or violent outbursts. Unexpressed and uncontrolled rage is dangerous. Train your child to express his feelings. Anger is a natural emotion that is full of energy. This energy can be constructively harnessed in an emergency. It is the intense unexpressed rage that is dangerous. Repressed rage is a monster that can be unleashed without warning. A person's rage can be triggered when he believes that he is being treated unjustly or when he feels disrespected. A person's rage can also be triggered when he is depressed, physically exhausted, or stressed. A person's rage can be triggered when he experiences panic anxiety. This is what happens in most road rage incidents. The monster of repressed rage is so powerful it will override all reason and all sense of control. As a parent, you must be able to detect repressed rage in your child so that you can help him avoid violent encounters. Train your child to be peaceful and loving. Help him learn to express himself through words, art, music, and sports. Encourage him to label his anger. Help him to identify the source of his rage and the trigger for his outbursts. Violent movies and violent video games are to be avoided. Do not shame or humiliate your child. As a parent, do not hit your child. Help him to build conscience and to develop empathy and compassion. Teach him to know the difference between right and wrong and to feel bad for his inappropriate behaviors. Your child must cultivate impulse control. Attachment to family is important. Build your child's self-esteem through success and praise. Have your child practice relaxing on a blanket every day. Encourage him to use positive self-talk to regulate his behaviors. Teach your child to love by loving him. The monster of repressed rage is so dangerous it can land a person in prison.

# THINK ON THESE THINGS

Your body will heal itself if you give it proper nutrition, proper exercise, proper rest, and proper joy. Your brain is your command and control center. Your brain will always try to fix whatever is wrong with your body. Your job is to assist your brain. Your mind will heal itself through joyful and loving experiences. Daily exercise and daily acts of kindness are effective therapies. Surround yourself with kind and caring friends and family members who can make a positive contribution to your life. Keep on being rational and physically healthy. A long-term loving relationship has healthy benefits. Sometimes you win and sometimes you lose. You do not have to win every time. People rarely die from old age. They almost always die from disease. Know your genetic patterns and invest in prevention. Cultivate a belief that you will live a long life. Life is precious. Live your life with a sense of urgency. Life is about limited time and the use of time. You have to take well calculated risks to obtain joy and fulfillment. Figure out what is for you and what is not for you. If golf is not for you, do not play golf. Take life one day at a time. Live a simple life. Learn to think for yourself. Remind your child to think for himself. Have a plan A and a plan B. Imitation is a basic way to learn. Teach your child to copy the good. We learn by trial and by error. Keep on trying. Learn from your mistakes and learn from the mistakes of others. Much of what everyone does is guesswork. Admitting that there is a lot that we do not know will reduce your anxiety and stress. Humans are more into self-preservation than self-sacrifice. The poor we will always have with us. Therefore, live a life full of compassion and kindness. You will reap whatever you sow. There are logical and natural consequences to the choices you make. Life is more predictable than we are willing to admit. You do not have to fix everything today. You can fix things as you go. There are talkers and there are doers. Many people with ability fail because they lack confidence. It takes a long time to build a structure. It takes a short time to break it down. Be part of a construct system. Never be part of a destruct system. There are many opinions but few facts. There is an upside and a downside to everything. From something bad can come something good. Look for the good. Consider all things carefully. If you do the same thing repeatedly, you will get the same results. Acquire knowledge for knowledge is power. What people say is mostly a projection of themselves. Many people talk too much and listen too little. Many people talk too much and observe too little. Many people are too involved with the outside world to be reflective. In the final analysis, your starting point is not that important. Neither are the bumps and bruises along the way. What really matters is where you end up. Many people do not recognize the darkness that is within their own souls. Be aware of it! The darkness is like a ninja. The moment you think you have it subdued, it is up, alive, and going again. Love is what you do. Always do your best. In the end, you can lead a horse to water but you cannot make it drink. You are not the savior of the world!

# THE RESERVED CHILD

Many children are reserved and would rather spend time at home than interact with the outside world. There is nothing wrong with being shy and quiet, although society appears to put more value on being outgoing. Many reserved children are highly internalized. Many of them function with great imagination and a rich inner life of thoughts, feelings, and fantasy. Accept your reserved child. Do not work to change him. If you accept your reserved child, he will learn to accept and value himself. Reserved does not mean weak. To be reserved is not a problem. A lack of essential life skills and low confidence is more of a problem. Help your child to explore and develop his strengths and his areas of interests. Teach him by words and by example to be assertive but not aggressive. Teach him to be a leader and not a follower. Teach him to be strong. Create many social experiences for your reserved child. Praise your reserved child for every success. Teach your reserved child social skills. Encourage him to be socially appropriate at all times. Never force your reserved child into uncomfortable social situations. Your reserved child may benefit from participation in acting, drama, and sports. Value his uniqueness. Your reserved child may be sensitive, reflective, observant, and bright. He may also be self-conscious with a measure of social anxiety. It is therefore important for your reserved child to express his feelings and learn to relax.

# A GREAT THINKER

There are many things that you can do to raise a great thinker who will not be gullible, easily manipulated, or victimized. In the first place, do not indoctrinate your child too heavily with your beliefs. Guide him with your suggestions delivered to him in an indirect manner. Encourage him to think for himself and to create his own ideas. There is not a whole lot that you need to teach a young child. The basics are to know the difference between right and wrong, to be compliant, to be socially appropriate, to sit still and complete a task, and to follow a simple schedule. Very early in his life, your child must understand the difference between beliefs and facts. He must also understand that some ideas are sensible and some ideas make no sense. Thoughts are not to be fully trusted. Thoughts come and thoughts go. Some are negative and silly and should be ignored. Negative thoughts can lead to negative emotions and negative behaviors. Some thoughts are not reality based. Encourage your child to entertain positive and realistic thoughts. Your child should not readily believe what other people say. There are many lies thrown around and there is a lot of misinformation in circulation. There are two sides to every story. Teach your child not to be gullible. Do not believe anything until you have had an opportunity to take it apart in an open-minded and critical manner. Engage your child in debates and discussions. Value his opinions. Introduce your child to brainstorming, cause and effect, problem definition, and problem solving. Teach your child the difference between opinions, beliefs, and scientific evidence. There is much that we do not know. The national news is biased and the sermons preached in church are projections from the preacher. It takes a rebellious attitude and a relaxed state of mind to become a great thinker. Encourage your child to keep an open mind and to be less rigid. Encourage your child to remain dedicated to reality and relative truth. Reinforce your child's thinking ability by responses such as "good thinking" or "you are a great thinker". Good sleep, daily exercise, and proper hydration will improve your child's ability to think. Becoming a great thinker comes with practice.

# SIBLING RIVALRY

A mild amount of sibling rivalry is normal and may even be healthy. Siblings who challenge each other may become stronger and more resilient. Through the process of give and take, siblings may improve their communication skills. They may also learn social skills and conflict resolution. There is a lot that parents can do to make sure that their children remain friends for life. First, we must understand that sibling rivalry is within the context of daily family life. Your children may be significantly different either in age or in personality. Do not practice any form of favoritism and do not encourage competition. Favoritism is dangerous. Do not put labels on your children such as the "smart one," or the "good one". Do not compare your children. They are different. Love them equally. Sometimes an older child will become threatened by the arrival of a new baby. That child will need reassurance that he is not being displaced. An older child may be recruited to do some things for the new baby. As a parent, encourage your children to negotiate and to compromise. It is much better when the children work out their differences by themselves. Give them time to do so before you get involved. No form of abuse should be tolerated. Strive to keep your home peaceful and stress-free as much as possible. Never allow sibling rivalry to escalate into violence which can have tragic consequences. No child should act as a parent. Do not allow bullying. It is important to be fair when you deal with your children. Fairness should be based on the needs of your children and not on their wants. When you plan family activities, consider the likes and dislikes of all the children. Individual time spent with each child is essential. Praise your children for their every success. It will build their self-esteem. Encourage team work. Parents should schedule regular family meetings when each child can express his concerns. Live by this mantra—"No matter what, we are family."

# THE DEPRESSED CHILD

Many children experience depression. Stress at home or at school can cause your child to become depressed. Some children may have suffered loss. Other children may have experienced emotional trauma such as bullying. Some children who battle chronic health problems may become depressed. Depression is defined as persistent sadness and inability to experience pleasure from potentially pleasurable activities. Your depressed child may exhibit reduced interest in his favorite activities. Be alert to a drop in your child's energy level. Your depressed child may become socially withdrawn. Some depressed children may be irritable and unable to properly concentrate. Some depressed children may experience a loss of appetite and some may display angry outbursts. Your depressed child may experience headaches, stomachaches, or sleep disturbance. A depressed child may engage in negative, hopeless talk and may fail to respond to humor. Depression in your child is serious. If you suspect that your child is depressed, immediately seek professional help for your child. Plan a range of joyful activities for your child. Take him outside for a walk out in nature. Help him to cultivate gratitude for what he has. The acquisition of essential life skills will help to make your child feel more competent and confident. Wholesome activities such as daily exercise, hobbies, and working on meaningful projects will help to keep him from becoming depressed. Encourage your child to perform kind deeds for others.

# THE NON-VERBAL CHILD

Most children acquire the ability to speak somewhere between the ages of one and three. Some children are simply late to talk. The non-verbal child, for a variety of reasons, does not use words to communicate. The non-verbal child will experience tension and frustration regarding his inability to produce words to communicate. In the case of a non-verbal child, it will be important to have his hearing checked. The major goal should be helping him find a way to communicate. Sessions with a speech pathologist may be helpful. As a parent, be observant of your non-verbal child, and take advantage of any attempts to communicate such as gestures, vocalizations, signs, and pictures. Your child may be well able to comprehend the spoken word. Check your child's language comprehension ability by asking him to respond to a simple request. If your child is not able to respond to your request, provide some practice by gently putting him through the activity in a physical manner. Talk to your non-verbal child and read to him. Ask him questions. Do not ignore your non-verbal child. Normalize him as much as possible. Secure solid eye contact with your non-verbal child when you speak to him. You can gently cup his face to establish eye contact. Provide ample opportunities for your child to play and interact socially. Read your child's non-verbal communication carefully. Do not create dependency by doing everything for him. Do not anticipate his wishes and simply hand things over to him. Encourage your child to communicate. Teach your non-verbal child to point out pictures. You may also teach him to exchange a picture for something that he wants. The ability to point out pictures and designs is an important skill that can be used to measure his non-verbal intelligence in the future. Suggest to your older non-verbal child to make pictures in his mind. Use soothing music to comfort your non-verbal child. Have him spend some quiet time on a blanket outdoors, where he can look at the trees and the clouds. Engage your non-verbal child in simple art activities such as drawing with crayons and using play dough. An older non-verbal child may be taught sign language. Keep your non-verbal child involved in fun activities so that he does not become withdrawn or depressed. Apply consequences in a fair, loving, and consistent manner. Your non-verbal child may become frustrated and angry. Give him a gentle hug until he is calm. Violence is not acceptable. Teach your non-verbal child to inhibit by the practice of responding to your instruction to stop. Physically demonstrate cause and effect to your child. Teach him abstract concepts in visual and physical ways. Routines will add predictability to his life and serve to reduce his stress. Give your non-verbal child daily backrubs. Strengthen his motor system through physical activities such as walking, running, and catching a soft ball. Get in touch with your local school regarding the use of technology for your non-verbal child.

# TOILET TRAINING
# YOUR CHILD

Do not rush your child. Bowel and bladder control are dependent on the neurological development of your child's motor system. Most children are not fully ready until age three. Make toilet training a pleasant experience. At first, anticipate and suggest. Always reinforce by offering praise or offering stickers for success. You may wish to have your child help to select a potty. Follow a regular toilet training schedule. If your child is dry at night and wet during the day, you should share this information with your child's pediatrician. If your older child is having difficulty mastering bowel and bladder control, you must first look at the problem from a physical viewpoint. Explore with your child's pediatrician the role of digestive problems. If there is no physical explanation, you should then consider the effect of stress. Bedwetting in children who are five years or older is not normal. If this happens, you should contact your child's pediatrician immediately. Persistent bedwetting may leave your child feeling out of control and embarrassed. It is not your child's fault and your child should never be punished for wetting the bed. Eventually your child will outgrow bedwetting as his neurological system matures. Have your child adopt the habit of using the bathroom before going to bed. Coach your child into attending to body sensations and needs. Your child can practice drinking water and holding for a few extra seconds when he needs to go. Make your child responsible for changing the wet bed sheets. Dry bed training involves waking the child up at intervals during the night to go to the bathroom. The downside to this method is that your child's sleep will be disturbed. As a parent, be warm, understanding, and patient. Soiling is a more serious problem than wetting and should be discussed with your child's pediatrician. If there is no physical explanation, you will need to consider the impact of stress. Remind your child to listen to his body. Praise every success. Let your child be responsible for cleaning himself up. In the case of chronic soiling, a change of clothing should be provided for your child when he is away from home.

# IMPROVING YOUR CHILD'S SLEEP

S ome children are poor sleepers. As a parent, recognize the importance of sleep. Through the process of sleeping the human body is repaired and restored. Your child's growth and development will be enhanced by quality sleep. Adequate sleep is also necessary for healthy immune functioning. When your child sleeps well, his brain functioning will be sharper and his emotions will be more positive. Your child will be better able to cope with daily demands. Take an individualized approach to your child's sleep. What may work for others may not work for your child. For some children, daily exercise is a must. Your child may not sleep properly if he is hungry. It is important to establish a regular sleep schedule for your child. Devote an hour before bedtime for your child to prepare for sleep. Teach him to relax before bedtime. There should be no television viewing and no significant brain work. Establish bedtime rituals such as a warm bath, a wholesome snack, a bedtime story, and a backrub. If your child wakes up every morning tired and grumpy, it is likely that he is not getting enough quality sleep. Behavior problems can be significantly reduced when a child gets proper sleep. The child who is sleeping well is more likely to function with good concentration and an alert mind. It is through the process of sleep that learning is cemented in your child's brain. Try to determine the ideal temperature and humidity of your home that will facilitate your child's sleep. Your child's mattress should be comfortable. Your child's room should be quiet. If your child is afraid of the dark, you should leave a night light on for him. Make sure that your home is safe and peaceful so that your child can feel secure. Always encourage your child to use the bathroom before going to bed. Do not give your child too many fluids before bedtime. Your child's intellectual, emotional, and behavioral functioning will improve when he gets enough quality sleep.

# DRUG PROOFING YOUR CHILD

As a parent, you are your child's first and most powerful teacher. Let your child know that his body is a wonderful machine that should be treasured. It is important to provide the body with balanced nutrition, daily exercise, proper hydration, joyful experiences, and quality sleep. In regards to drugs, there are illicit drugs, prescription drugs, and over the counter drugs. Illicit drugs are highly addictive and illegal. You can go to prison for making, selling, buying, or using illicit drugs. Prescription drugs are made by pharmaceutical companies and prescribed by medical personnel. They are often used to treat disease. Do not overuse over the counter or prescription drugs, and have nothing to do with illicit drugs. Be a good example to your child of healthy living. Your child will copy you. Do not take medication for every minor ailment. In many cases, your body will heal itself if you give it proper nutrition, daily exercise, pure water, joyful experiences, and adequate sleep. Drugs have adverse side effects. Your child should learn to manage his stress and learn to use natural and healthy approaches to improve his health. Guide your child into cultivating a sound philosophy of healthy living. Encourage him to engage in wholesome social activities with friends and family members who are a good influence on him. Teach your child to think for himself. Encourage independent functioning and assertiveness. Your child must learn to stand up to social pressure. Teach your child to value his health. Involve your child in sports and encourage him to exercise daily in the great outdoors.

# PARENTING AND MARRIAGE

P arenting is one of the most difficult jobs you will ever face. Different children require different approaches. There are many opinions floating around and advice is everywhere. As a parent, there will be times when you will not know which way to go. Should you be firm or should you be lenient? Trust your parental instinct, and rely on your knowledge and sound judgement. Approach your child with care and warmth. Use simple language and keep the interaction loving and enjoyable. Create fond memories. Follow your child's lead at times and engage him in his chosen activities when appropriate. A good parent is firm, loving, and full of praise. Grab every opportunity to teach kindness, compassion, vocabulary, and thinking skills. Parenting should be an emotional experience. Do not pressure your child. Let him develop at his own speed. Allow many opportunities for self-expression and free play. A child raised within the context of a good marriage is a lucky child. Marriage, under the best of circumstances, is challenging but not impossible. Marriage requires communication, negotiation, and a great deal of compromise. Do not go crazy grieving for the perfect union that you do not have when you wake up to the deficits in your spouse. Be realistic with your expectations and remember that you are not perfect either. You have a choice. You can either dwell on the good stuff or dwell on the not so good stuff. Focus on self-improvement. Take the time to calculate the impact you are having on your spouse. Never allow yourself to become too dependent on your partner. Marriage is hard work. Be a team player and always approach your spouse with kindness and respect.

# IMAGINE AND PRETEND

Engage your child in imaginative and pretend play. Show your child a large picture that tells a story. While your child is looking at the picture, tell him the story. Ask him to close his eyes and pretend that he is part of the story. Imaginative and pretend play will build your child's intellect, creativity, and confidence. Through imaginative play and pretend activities, your child will learn about the workings of the real world. Your child can pretend to be a doctor or a nurse. Your child can make mud pies for sale. Your child can pretend to be an explorer. Your child can pretend to operate a grocery store. Your child can pretend to be a gardener. He can make believe that he is going camping. Imaginative and pretend play will be great fun for your child. Ask him "What would happen if…." or "What would you do if…." While you are involved in imaginative play and pretend activities with your child, take the time to demonstrate abstract concepts such as slow, fast, above, and below. Through imaginative and pretend activities, your child will learn to put himself in the place of another. This will help him to develop empathy and compassion and help to build his conscience.

# PSYCHIATRIC DIAGNOSES

Psychiatric disorders are not medical diseases. There are no lab tests, X-rays, brain scans, or chemical imbalance measures that are used to verify the existence of a mental disorder. Psychiatric labels are applied to clusters of emotions and behaviors in a somewhat subjective manner. Psychiatric labels then take on a life of their own and soon people are treated as if they have a disease. In many cases, interviews and observations form the basis of the diagnosis. Psychometric testing is sometimes done. Psychiatric labels facilitate communication between professionals and they are often required for third party payment. Psychiatric labels help to define the problem and they serve to describe the presenting symptoms. On the other hand, psychiatric labels may add to the stigma of mental illness. In some cases, people who are given a psychiatric label are prescribed medication that may produce adverse side effects. Psychiatric disorders are often ranked as mild, moderate, or severe. Some psychiatric conditions are connected to physical disorders. In other cases, a person's psychiatric disorder may result from a life of emotional trauma.

# EXCEPTIONAL EDUCATION

Exceptional education is a school program designed for students with significant physical, learning, and behavioral disabilities. Students with mild impairments should be educated with their peers in a regular education classroom. Impairments may be in the areas of physical development, intellectual development, social-emotional development, language development, or communication skills. Children who are autistic, developmentally delayed, learning disabled, or intellectually impaired will benefit greatly from early intervention. Some of these children will need physical therapy, occupational therapy, or speech and language therapy. It is especially important to teach a child with a disability to be socially appropriate. Help him to learn compliance to authority and help him to develop impulse control. The stress of raising a child with a significant disability is enormous. Many parents grieve for the perfect child they do not have. Some of these parents will become depressed or angry. Exceptional education comes with negative labels. Hopefully, the special services provided are well worth the label. A disabled child who is reserved should not be placed in a classroom that is filled with severely disabled, aggressive children. The modeling effect will be extremely negative. A well-designed, individualized education program should be in place for all students. As a parent, there is plenty that you can do to help your child on the home front. Teach your child about safety. Make sure that he is compliant. Teach him to sit still and complete a simple task. Use a series of pictures to develop his visual memory. Have daily conversations with your child. Ask him a series of questions. Have him watch educational videos. Teach your child to follow a simple schedule. When you read stories to your child and when you tell stories to your child, encourage him to form pictures in his mind regarding the story. Help him to improve his reading skills through daily practice.

# THE SLOW LEARNER

A slow learner is a child who functions with low average intelligence and who is struggling to keep up with age and grade level academic tasks. A slow learner can learn but at a slower rate. A person's Intelligence can change over time. It is therefore possible that a slow learner can become an average or above-average student. A slow learner may go through the normal stages of development like all children but at a slower pace. Do not retain the slow learner in his grade. Plan an individualized program for him based on his strengths and interests. At the beginning, it will be more productive to teach the slow learner in concrete and visual ways. As he gets older, emphasize abstract concepts taught through physical demonstrations and pictures. For example, show the slow learner a table. Have him see and touch the table. Next, place your hand above the table and let him watch. Explain the concept of above the table while he looks on. Next, place your hand below the table. Explain the concept of below the table to him. Break down every task that you wish to teach the slow learner into small steps. Teach him with repeated practice and immediate reinforcement through verbal praise. Your slow learner is likely to experience high anxiety. Provide for frequent breaks and exercise. Let him spend some time outdoors every day. Have him lie on a blanket and experience relaxation through quiet time. Normalize the slow learner by treating him in normal ways. Help him to develop essential life skills. Success and praise will build his confidence. Give your slow learner a way to learn. Turn him into a powerful visual learner through visual memory practice and through visual reasoning practice. Help your slow learner to master the sounds of the alphabet so that he can become a good reader. Engage him in phonetic practice using simple nonsense words. Involve your slow learner in hands-on projects at home while you demonstrate and explain. Be an effective and involved parent. In the classroom, your slow learner should be seated up front. It will be important to get his attention before giving him instructions. Do not give the slow learner homework. Every attempt should be made to have the slow learner complete his academic work in school where assistance is available. Evenings should be reserved for family time which may include conversations, educational videos, and free reading. Teach your slow learner to write a simple sentence. Encourage independent functioning by having your slow learner do things for himself. As a parent, work closely with the classroom teacher and school principal. A true measure of an effective school is that school's ability to turn a slow learner into an above-average student.

# AUDITORY PROCESSING DISORDER

Children who are diagnosed with an auditory processing disorder experience difficulty attending to the spoken word, understanding the spoken word, and remembering the spoken word. It is entirely a brain processing disorder. The first thing a parent should do if you suspect that your child has an auditory processing problem is to have an audiologist evaluate your child's hearing. If your child has good hearing, and still cannot properly understand and respond to the spoken word, your child may have an auditory processing disorder. The comprehension of abstract words may be especially difficult. You can build your child's abstract vocabulary by explaining abstract words in concrete, visual, and hands-on ways. Attention, concentration, and auditory memory may be enhanced through the practice of listening to and repeating back a series of random numbers. Expressive language can be improved through social experiences and daily conversations. Auditory processing involves attending to what you hear, understanding what you hear, remembering what you hear, and producing correct responses in verbal or written form. As a parent, you may have to repeat yourself to your child. Teach him to picture scenarios in his mind. Imaginary and pretend activities will help to improve your child's ability with the comprehension of abstract concepts. Some children who experience high anxiety may display patterns that resemble auditory processing disorder. Teach your child to slow down, calm down, and relax.

# ATTENTION DEFICIT
# HYPERACTIVE DISORDER

C hildren with ADHD will find it difficult to attend to a task. They often fail to inhibit their impulses, and may experience difficulty completing an assignment. ADHD children often display poor planning and they often function in a disorganized manner. Your ADHD child may display a tremendous need to move and touch. A high energy child is not necessarily an ADHD child. The child with ADHD may have a weak motor system which helps to explain impulsivity, poor focus, and weak concentration. Physical activity will help to strengthen his motor system. The child with ADHD will have a hard time stopping himself. Medication is often prescribed for children who are diagnosed with ADHD. These drugs may produce serious side effects such as weight gain, violent outbursts, and depression. Drugs may also cause a child to lose touch with his authentic self. If your child is active and hard to control, begin to train his motor system. Have him practice impulse control. He must learn to stop himself on your command and then be able to stop himself on his own command. Have your child practice task completion in a timely manner. For the ADHD child, create a low-stress environment. Routines and schedules will help to add structure and predictability to your child's life. Have him practice relaxation by lying on a blanket for quiet time. Make sure your ADHD child gets enough daily exercise and proper sleep. Be consistent and firm with behavior management. Train your ADHD child to be socially appropriate at all times. Be firm, yet loving. Apply consequences in a consistent manner. Work hard to manage your ADHD child without drugs.

# ADVOCATING FOR
# YOUR CHILD

As a parent, you need to be a strong advocate for your child. Be assertive and wise. There is a great deal that is negotiable. Be indirect and non-threatening in your dealings with professionals. Cultivate the people you respect. You may need the support of a trusted friend. Team up with competent and caring people that you trust. In the school system, there are professionals such as school counselors, school social workers, and school psychologists who are child advocates. Do not practice denial. Be in touch with your own depression and your own anger. You may find it hard to see the problem for what it is because of your closeness to the situation. Trust your instincts. Good parents are well tuned in to their children and they are often correct. Your two most important goals should be to properly define your child's problem and to develop an appropriate individualized intervention program. If your child needs to be evaluated ask questions regarding the qualifications of the evaluator. Seek out professionals who are well trained and who possess extensive experience. Learn all you can about the presenting problem. Do your research and write everything down in a notebook. Solicit the input of the classroom teacher when you are dealing with an academic or behavior problem. When you are dealing with a behavior management problem you should get the school principal involved. You must advocate for your child with urgency if you suspect that your child is being bullied or abused. Be a strong advocate for your child.

# YOUR CHILD AND SPORTS

D o not force your child into sports. Encourage him. There are many benefits to playing sports and there are many life lessons to be learned. Be an active family. Spend time outdoors. Go for walks. Do some jogging. Ride your bikes. Play catch. Hit a tennis ball with a plastic bat and run the bases. Watch some sports on television. Your child may decide that he wants to play little league baseball. Make sure that his coach is a kind, patient, trustworthy, and caring person. Sports should be for enjoyment, social experience, and exercise. Through sports your child will improve his motor skills and become more rhythmic, more coordinated, and more controlled. Through team sports your child will make new friends, learn about team work, and further develop his social skills. Engaging in sports will teach your child how to win and how to lose. Encourage your child to enjoy the process and not be overly focused on the outcome. Good sportsmanship is important to learn. Sports is a way to enhance body image and self-esteem. Playing sports will lower your child's anxiety level and bring him great joy. Sports will teach your child to be mentally tough, confident, and resilient.

# THE IMPORTANCE OF PLAY

Have you ever taken the time to observe children at play? It is total joy. Engage your child in playful activities from the beginning. Unstructured, but well supervised play can be a lot of fun for your young child. An older child may enjoy structured play which will introduce him to the idea of organization and compliance with rules. Establish good eye contact as you play with your child. Use simple language but do not engage in baby talk. Do not tickle your baby. He is not able to tell you to stop when the stimulation is too much. Games such as "Now you see it, now you don't" can be a start. Place the baby on a soft blanket. Cuddle the baby in a gentle way and talk to him. Play enhances attachment. Play is a source of happiness. Through play, your child will learn to interact with others and learn to express himself. Play will serve as a release for pent up feelings. Through play activities, your child will be stimulated and inspired. His motor skills, his language ability, and his visual-spatial functioning will improve. Engage your older child in an ongoing conversation while he is playing. Give him the chance to voice his opinions. Play will build creativity, increase resiliency, and enhance confidence. Through play your child will learn to overcome his fears. Through play your child will engage in problem solving and the release of tension. Group play will teach your child to share and to get along with others. Through properly supervised play, your child will refine his social skills. Through play, your child will learn to win and at the same time learn to accept defeat. Through play your child will begin to make the connection between fantasy and reality. Play will help your child to improve his attention span while offering many opportunities for experimentation, imagination, and pretend. Play activities will provide for exercise which may improve your child's behaviors and sleep. Children who play outside may develop a love for nature. Childhood play will create fond memories which will serve as cushions when tough times come. Play activity is good preparation for adult living. As your child gets older, let him know that work must come before play the way dinner must come before dessert. Always supervise your child at play and think safety.

# YOUR CHILD'S BODY IMAGE

Help your child to develop a healthy body image. You can either love your body or you can hate your body. Body image is about one's perception of physical attractiveness and self-worth. A person's body image has much to do with happiness and self-confidence now and in the future. Help your child to accept and love his unique body. Be a good role model for your child. Do not speak negatively about your body in front of him. Do not express dissatisfaction with your body and do not compare your body with others. Resist the many messages from celebrities and social media regarding the perfect or ideal body. It is important to take care of your body so that it can perform well. Take your child outdoors. Have him walk and run for fun. This will improve his strength, coordination, and speed. Let your child know that you value good health which has much to do with healthy eating, proper sleep, pure water, and daily exercise. Never tell your child that he is fat. Your child will go through important body changes as he grows up. Educate him so that he knows what to expect. The concept of sexual attractiveness should not be overemphasized. Always remind your child of his strengths and of his interests. Instead of being stuck on himself, teach your child to do kind deeds for others. There is no such thing as the perfect body. Remind your child that his body is a wonderful machine that is the source of great joy when it is working right. His job is to love his body and take good care of it.

# LEARN TO BE HAPPY

Happiness will not simply descend upon you. It is up to you to create happiness for yourself and for your child. Happiness is not the costly trip to Europe or the exciting cruise to the Caribbean. Happiness is the accumulation of daily happy events. Money contributes to happiness but happiness is much more than money. Make sure that you are physically and mentally well. The basics are healthy nutrition, daily exercise, proper sleep, pure water, joyful activities, and freedom from stress. Make sure that your body is working right. Encourage your child in his areas of strengths and his passions. Teach your child to accept and value himself. You are not perfect and neither is your child. Accept him for who he is. Keep it simple. Praise your child often. Call him by his name for his name is special. Allow many opportunities for free play. Explore some new activities. Stick with the ones you enjoy. Daily acts of kindness and generosity will bring you great joy. Do your best and learn to be content. Count your blessings daily. Encourage your child to do his best and to accept the outcome after his best effort. Family activities such as cookouts are great fun. Help your child to pursue a hobby and encourage him to play sports. Cultivate a sense of humor and do not take life too seriously. Do not overschedule. Know what activities make you happy and have the courage and discipline to pursue them. Live your life one happy day at a time. Do not communicate your anxieties to your child. Many of the things that we worry about never happen. Sing and dance. Tell some jokes and laugh out loud. Take your child for a walk out in nature. Look at a lovely sunset or go for a walk on the beach. Let go of your traumatic past but cling to the good memories. Fun times will come again. Create some happiness.

# LET YOUR BABY GROW UP

B abies are warm, soft, and cuddly. Your baby is a source of love and joy, but your baby is not here to meet your emotional needs. Let your baby grow up! The warmth, love, and joy that you get from your baby should not be the focus. You should continue to have your emotional needs for attention, affection, and self-worth met through your interactions with the adults in your life. If your baby is your only source of affection, that would be sad. The relationship with your baby is mostly a one-way street. Protect, love, and nurture your baby without seeking anything in return. Over time, your baby will respond to you with eye contact, smiles, hugs, and kisses. This is a normal and natural response to your loving care. Your baby will be needy and dependent. He will make you feel important, needed, and powerful. It will be easy to boss this little person around. The long-term goal is to have your child grow up to become a loving, competent, and independent adult. Parenting is essentially a painful process of separation. Your child must be able to separate from you and learn to function in the real world. Do not allow your personhood to become fused with that of your baby. From the beginning, help your child to acquire the essential life skills that will enable him to become independent. Real life demands that you take some well calculated risks even though you desire to protect your child. Your baby must slowly become his own person. Your baby must gradually become his authentic and differentiated self. Let your baby grow up.

# RAISING YOUR CHILD'S INTELLIGENCE

Intelligence is the ability to think and reason. General intelligence is determined by genetics, intellectual/sensory stimulation, and social-emotional nurturing. Some people will tell you that intelligence is fixed. This is not true. You can increase your child's intelligence. Your child's intelligence level can also decline because of brain damage or physical disease. Make sure that your child is physically healthy and that he always receives proper nutrition, adequate sleep, pure water, and daily exercise. He must learn to protect his brain at all times. Keep his life stress-free as much as possible. Pay attention to allergies and digestive functioning. Science is consistently pointing towards a connection between gut health and brain health. Talk to your child and read to your child. Provide a loving environment for him. Take your child on field trips. Point out details to him. Engage your older child in exercises that will build his auditory and visual memory. Have him listen to and repeat back a series of random numbers. Have him recall and describe visual images that were shown to him. As your child gets older, introduce him to abstract vocabulary such as above and below. Teach your child about cause-effect relationships, problem definition, and problem solving. Make learning fun. Ask your child for his opinions and include him in brainstorming sessions. Daily conversations will help to build his intellect. Present "what would you do if....."

scenarios to him for his input. Expose your child to music and help him develop his writing skills. Get your child on a reading program. Encourage him to read on a variety of challenging topics. Success and praise will build your child's confidence. Invest in some educational toys and use the computer for extra cognitive and academic practice. Daily exercise and sports will help to keep your child's mind sharp. Stimulate his senses through age-appropriate fun activities. Let him experience a variety of textures, tastes, smells, sights, and sounds. Encourage your child to relax so that he can function with a calm mind. Unstructured play will help to build your child's creativity. Consistently praise your child's ability to think. Your older child will benefit from having conversations with great thinkers who create new ideas.

# THE KEY TO SUCCESS

There are many who believe that intelligence is the key to success. That may be somewhat true since intelligence and academic achievement are highly related. A fair amount of intelligence is required to establish realistic goals, to create and execute a game plan, and to learn the things that you need to learn. There is something that is perhaps more important than intelligence when we are talking about achievement. Some people call it inner strength or strong desire. Some people define it as perseverance or resiliency. Some people call it grit or mental toughness. Some people call it willpower. There are those who refer to this inner quality as the fighter in you. There is no substitute for inner drive and hard work. Encourage your child to never give up. When the task is challenging, encourage him to be independent, hardworking, and strong. Help is always available if needed. Keep moving forward. Teach your child to believe in himself. Encourage him to visualize success. As a parent, model true grit to your child. Let him face some challenges and let him learn from every failure. Raise your child to be rugged in his efforts and gentle in his dealings. It is all about that strong inner drive to achieve.

# AUTISM DISORDER

Autism Disorder is a neurological developmental disorder that is usually manifested by age three. Functional deficits can be mild, moderate, or severe. The autistic child may experience significant difficulty with speech articulation and the understanding of language. In many cases, motor system deficits are also present. Autistic children may find it hard to acquire age and grade level academic skills. The autistic child may display a range of frustration-type behaviors, as well as inappropriate social behaviors when interacting with his peers. The autistic child may prefer to play by himself. He may exhibit repetitive, self-stimulating behaviors such as hand flapping, head banging, and rocking. Autistic children may display a range of behaviors that lack purpose. Many autistic children are not socially and emotionally responsive. Many are rigid and lacking in empathy. The autistic child may display frequent temper tantrums and a range of odd behaviors. As the parent of an autistic child, there is much that you can do at home to help him. Your approach to teaching him simple skills should be concrete and highly visual, with much repetition and rapid reinforcement through verbal praise. Break down the task you wish to teach him into small steps. The autistic child will benefit from early intervention and from a range of services which may include occupational therapy, speech and language therapy, and social skills training. As a parent, get your autistic child involved in community activities and field trips. Allow him to mingle with other autistic children as well as non-autistic children. Explore the range of services that are offered by your local school. Seek out someone whom you respect and trust to serve as an advocate. You will need to take breaks from the stress of raising your autistic child. Join a parent group. Give your autistic child frequent backrubs. Have him engage in daily exercise. Introduce him to soothing music. Be on the alert for sensitivity to loud noise. Follow a daily schedule and keep routines in place. Frequent hugs will provide contact comfort and a sense of security. As a parent, teach your autistic child to be compliant, peaceful, and socially appropriate. Do not tolerate physical or verbal aggression from your autistic child.

# TEST TAKING SKILLS

N ever tell your child that you were a poor student or a poor test-taker when you were in school. You will only raise his anxiety level regarding academic performance and specifically test taking. Do not tell your child that you had math phobia. Your child should get into the habit of studying hard and preparing well for every academic test. From an early age, train your child to take tests. Provide the practice. Construct simple math and spelling tests for your child to complete at home. Let your child become familiar with the idea of taking a test. Make it fun. When your child returns from school, let him know that you have prepared a fun test for him to take. Praise his performance. Test taking will soon become second nature. In regards to a classroom test, your child must know what the test will cover. He must know how to prepare. Remind your child to relax and to do his best. Positive self-talk is important. If your child is well prepared, all he needs to think is "relax and do my best." To prepare for a timed test, your child should practice timed copying at home. Have him copy letters or numbers as fast as he can. Make it a game and make it fun. This will help to build his concentration and speed of performance. Never accept poor quality work from your child. Do not help him with tasks that he can complete on his own. Tell your child not to fight hard to remember the material when taking a test. Encourage him to relax and allow the knowledge he has to flow. Make sure your child gets to bed early the night before a test. Teach your child to lower his anxiety level through relaxation and by slow, long, deep, breathing. If your child is nervous about math, tell him that people invented math to help them transact real-life business such as adding, dividing, and measuring things.

# POWER OVER YOU

It is important to teach your child that words are just words and that opinions are only opinions. The words spoken by others and the opinions that they hold may not be based on facts. Do not give people power over you. Your child needs to grow up to be strong and assertive. Your child must learn to perform from a place of internal control. He should not be controlled by the environment. Help your child to cultivate inner strength. Your child must know the difference between right and wrong and he must learn to respect and obey legitimate adult authority. Teach your child not to worry about what people think or say about him. People may choose to like you or they may choose to dislike you. Be who you are. Once you are loved by your family and your friends you will be fine. Love yourself and you will be fine. You have no control over what people think, say, or do. As a parent, do not raise a child that is too passive or too aggressive. Raise a child who is full of inner strength. Teach your child to be assertive and effective. A reserved child can be strong. A kind child can be intelligent. As a parent, be a good example of inner strength, assertiveness, and kindness. Your child should never allow others to take advantage of him. Do not be like the giving tree that gave everything. Learn to say no when it is appropriate to say no. Teach your child to walk away from criticism, abuse, and confrontation. Teach your child to pick his friends carefully. Teach your child to value and respect all people. Teach your child to think for himself. As your child gets older, have conversations with him about healthy relationships, privacy, and boundaries. Teach your child to only assign credibility to people who earn it and deserve it. Do not give people power over you.

# DOING THE OPPOSITE

Help your child to experience a balanced development by sometimes doing the opposite. For the concrete learner, teach him abstract vocabulary. For the highly intelligent child, assign him some household chores and help him develop empathy and compassion. If your child is an outdoors person have him spend some time indoors, reading and reflecting. If your child is stuck indoors, take him outside for a hike in nature. For the rigid child, promote flexibility by giving him some choices. For the loud and boisterous child, have him lie on a blanket for some quiet time. For the quiet and reserved child, activate him with some loudness and jokes. For the frightened child, let him see you being brave and strong. Comfort the frightened child so that he feels safe and secure. For the dependent child, only provide help when he absolutely needs help. For the highly independent child, offer to help him. If your child does not talk much, engage him in conversation. If your child talks too much, have him listen to some music with you. If your child does everything in a fast manner, tell him to slow down when he talks, when he walks, and when he eats. For the socially inappropriate child, you the parent, must always demonstrate socially appropriate behaviors. For the reckless child, emphasize safety. If your child is angry and aggressive, emphasize peacefulness and self-control. For the depressed child, surround him with joyful and exciting activities. For the mentally weak child, be an example of inner strength. Provide him with some challenges. For the child who is unstructured, have him play an organized game with clear rules. For the structured child, let him engage in play activities of his own choosing. You can help your child by sometimes doing the opposite.

# TOWARDS AN
# ACCURATE DIAGNOSIS

I f you suspect that your child has a problem, it is important that you obtain an accurate diagnosis. Differential diagnosis is always a challenge because some conditions mimic each other. An example of this is hyperactivity and anxiety. A diagnostic label facilitates communication between professionals and it helps to define the problem. A diagnostic label may be necessary to obtain services and financial support for your child. Diagnostic work is good detective work that may include interviews, observations, psychological testing, and medical evaluations. A good evaluator is rational and conservative in his approach. Good diagnostic work is both art and science. There are many competent professionals available to you. Inquire about their training and experience. Do your homework. A good examiner will chase down every hypothesis and rule out all possibilities until he finds something that he cannot dismiss. A private evaluation is not necessarily superior to one that is offered by an agency or school. Do not be overly impressed by lengthy reports and technical terms. Keep in mind that the accuracy of your child's report findings and test scores may be threatened by factors such as your child's high anxiety level and fear of the examiner. It is easy to obtain medical and psychological test scores. It takes high level training, years of experience, and rational thinking to properly interpret test results. Clinical impressions are as valid as test scores. The most accurate diagnostic conclusion is reached when great diagnostic minds converge. It is through a meeting of the minds of rational, knowledgeable, and experienced professionals that an accurate diagnosis is achieved.

# KNOWING THE CAUSE

Knowing the cause of your child's problem may have some benefit when you are designing an intervention plan. The most realistic possibilities are genetic predisposition, brain disorder, emotional trauma, and ineffective parenting. If your child's problem is caused by a physical condition, his intervention plan may involve medical personnel. If your child's problem was caused by emotional trauma or ineffective parenting, your child will have to be treated within the context of his family. Parents will have to be part of the treatment program. More important than learning about the cause is knowing the nature and severity of the problem and designing a proper intervention plan that will resolve the mal-adaptive behavior. As a parent, know that there are many well trained, caring, and experienced professionals available to you.

# COPING SKILLS

The world is a tough place. Your child will face many challenges. He will experience failure, losses, and abuse. Help your child to develop strong coping skills. Teach him to be mentally tough and to be resilient. Teach your child to be assertive and to say "No" when it is appropriate to do so. Encourage your child to learn from every failure. Teach your child to respect authority and to cultivate impulse control. Train your child to be socially appropriate. Encourage your child to be rational and to always make sense. Train him to think for himself. Teach your child to be independent and to never give up. Teach your child the difference between a crisis and a small problem. Teach your child to walk away from a confrontation and not allow it to escalate. In his life, your child will experience some suffering. Teach your child to use positive realistic self-talk to structure and encourage himself. Teach him to name his fears. Help your child to create good memories. Good memories give us hope for the future. Introduce the words courage and perseverance to your older child. He will be strong if you are strong. Try to reduce the stress on him. Have your child practice relaxation by lying on a blanket for quiet time and by listening to soft, soothing music. Teach your child not to personalize the opinions of others. Vigorous daily exercise will improve his sleep and his coping ability. The more essential life skills your child develops, the more confident he will become.

# THE ONLY CHILD

Sometimes, the decision to have an only child is made because of economic reasons. The cost of raising and educating a child is enormous. A new parent may also realize that they are lacking in parenting skills and conclude that the challenge of raising one child is sufficient. Sometimes, family members will put pressure on the parents of an only child to have more children. It is the parent's choice to make. Many only children turn out to be well adjusted, bright, and high achieving. In the case of an only child, the full energy and direct attention of his parents may be overwhelming. Therefore, as the parent of an only child, be indirect with him much of the time. Praise him often for his good behaviors and apply consequences in a consistent manner. Your only child will spend a great deal of time in adult company. Do not allow him to act like an adult. Shield him from the stress of adult conversations. In a gentle manner, remind him that he is a child. Provide many opportunities for social experiences. Play dates will help him to develop the skills of sharing and team work. Your only child will likely have an advanced vocabulary. Help him to develop his fine and gross motor skills through activities such as tracing, copying, walking, and running. Allow your only child to become independent and therefore well able to separate from you. Encourage him to think for himself. Let him assist with family projects. As he gets older, assign him a daily chore. Teach him about privacy and social boundaries. Teach him to be socially appropriate. Do not overindulge. Do not pay him for doing every little job. Teach your only child to know the difference between right and wrong and to develop empathy and compassion. Your only child may feel lonely sometimes. Play catch with him or watch a movie together. Teach your only child about conflict resolution and teach him to be kind and compassionate. Encourage your only child to forge his own identity based on his strengths and his passions. Your only child will benefit from membership in a group or club that is well organized and operated by people you can fully trust.

# SOMETHING TO CONNECT TO

A child's internal life is a combination of what he has been taught and what he has experienced. Teach your child many wholesome ideas and give him rich and positive experiences. Life is difficult. The world is a challenging place. Many children will be overcome by anxiety triggered by the demands of home and school. Your child will need to feel connected. As a parent, commit yourself to the practice of realistic and positive thinking. It will be something for your child to connect to. Cuddle your child and tell him that you love him so that he will have your warm feelings to connect to. Help your child to know the difference between right and wrong. Kindness, empathy, and compassion will be something to connect to. Let your child see you doing kind deeds for others. It will be something to connect to. Give your child the gift of friendship so that he will have a positive relationship to connect to. Give your child fond memories and great experiences so that he will have something hopeful to connect to. Start some family traditions such as cookouts and going for walks on the beach. Play and laugh with your child so that he will feel connected. Success experiences will be something that he will definitely connect to.

# POSITIVE AND
# REALISTIC SELF-TALK

As your child gets older, teach him to use his silent inner language to structure and encourage himself. He does not need to speak out loud. Let him learn to use his silent inner language to effectively guide himself through a variety of situations. In his mind, he can say "stop" or "walk away" to control himself and prevent escalation. He can say to himself "relax" to calm his mind. Your child can learn to say "slower" for self-regulation and he can learn to say "faster" to speed up. Positive and realistic self-talk will become your child's internal guidance system. Positive and realistic self-talk will help your child to execute motor skills with confidence. Negative self-talk used by your child is self-defeating. Instead of saying "I'll try," your child should say to himself "I will." Instead of saying "I can't" he should say "I can." As your child gets older, his self-talk will become more sophisticated. "Never create an opportunity for me to become a victim," is a good example. Positive and realistic self-talk will help to conquer negative thoughts and depression. Positive and realistic self-talk will guide your child into making good choices and help him to control his bad urges.

# TO RESPOND AND TO INITIATE

From the beginning, encourage your baby to respond. Give him good eye contact as you speak to him. Praise his every response. Make the vocal sounds that your child makes. Imitate your child and let your child imitate you. As your child gets older, engage him in more sophisticated activities. Pause now and then to allow him to respond. Give respect to your child. Take time to listen. Give your child a chance to speak. At first, he may not be able to provide good verbal responses. Coach him and help him to formulate a good language response. Help your child to develop a good vocabulary. Teach him the meaning of words. Work from a basic word list. Introduce new ideas to your child. It is important for him to learn to say, "Thank you" and "Please." It is important for your child to promptly stop when you ask him to stop. It is important for your child to promptly come when you ask him to come. When your child initiates on his own, he is functioning at a much higher level than when he simply responds. Provide your older child with supplies such as large sheets of construction paper, crayons, and building blocks. At first you may have to help him build things. Provide a stimulating environment. Then, sit back and allow him to initiate. Whenever your child initiates, be quick to respond with praise. Say, "Good job!" When you praise your child, he will become more skilled and more confident. A skilled and confident child will initiate more and more. When you engage your child in motor activities such as crawling, walking, and running, you are helping your child to develop the ability to respond and initiate. Let your child run and play. At school, your child should have long periods of school recess so that he can move freely. Let your child's motor system flourish so that he can better respond and initiate. Train your child to be effective. Encourage your child to make things happen instead of simply allowing things to happen to him.

# TEACH YOUR CHILD TO FEEL

Developing your child's ability to feel is one of the important jobs of parenting. It is often overlooked because of the belief that children learn to feel on their own. As a parent, be warm, emotional, and nurturing. You are your child's best example and teacher. Let your child see you laugh and let your child see you cry. Let your child know that you sometimes feel sad, frustrated, frightened, and angry. Robotic, mechanical, and intellectual approaches will not help your child to grow emotionally. Be a touchy, feely person, who is lavish with praise, and generous with hugs, kisses, and backrubs. Call your child's name and tell him that you love him many times every day. Sometimes you can simply call him love. Whisper it in his ears and it will become stored in his mind. Talk about feelings. Help your child to identify and label his feelings. Are you feeling happy? Are you feeling sad? Are you feeling angry? Are you scared? Engage your child in conversation. Ask him, "How would you feel if…." questions. Apologize to your child when you hurt his feelings. Let your child know that his poor behaviors hurt your feelings. Talk about the feelings of the characters in stories that you read to him. Sings songs that are laden with emotional words. Let your child use his words to express his feelings in a guided and controlled manner. Let him know that feelings are the rich part of our lives.

# RESPECT YOUR CHILD

Your child is sacred. Approach him with reverence. Let respect be a major part of your family life. Your child has rights and he has feelings. He is a unique individual and not a carbon copy of you. Get to know your child and learn to delight yourself in his special traits and talents. As a parent, be a good example of respect towards others. When you interact with your child, be gentle in your approach. When you make a mistake, apologize to your child. Really listen to what he is trying to communicate to you. Value his likes and dislikes and allow him to make choices some of the time. Respect his personal boundaries and privacy except when he is at risk. Instill in your child good manners and politeness. Teach him to be considerate of others. Be a role model for what is socially appropriate. Express appreciation to your child. Call him by his name for his name is special. Let your child learn to do things for himself. Do not force your child to give hugs or to share his belongings. Respect his wishes. Talk to him about being loving and kind and let him decide. As you respect your child, he will learn to respect you.

# FUN WITH YOUR CHILD

Have fun with your child. Do not take life so seriously. Before you know it, life is over. Lighten up. Do not be so rigid and controlling. Laugh a little and laugh out loud. Life is not only about work. You do not have to be productive all day long. Play games with your child. Sing and dance. You can play catch with an older child. Take time to be silly. Tell him some jokes. Cookouts and campouts will give your child a sense of adventure and bring him much pleasure. Be creative. Start some family traditions. Bring joy to your child. Get a small tent and camp out in the backyard. Take your child for a walk on the beach. It is fun doing kind deeds for the neighbors. Plan family gatherings where there is good food and lively music. Take your child to the zoo. Work on a project together. Help your child with his chores. Be a fun person. Do not scold your child for spilling his drink or for accidentally breaking a glass. Just clean it up. Life is like that. Go for walks in the park. Hug your child often and roll around on the grass. Have some fun. Buy surprises for your child now and then. Take time to play exactly what your child wants to play. Share the adventures of your own childhood with him. Schedule daily fun with your child. When he is older, he will look back and remember with fondness all the fun he had when he was a child.

# YOUR ADOPTED CHILD

The adoption of a child is a loving act and a wonderful event. A child should be told from the beginning that he is adopted. The idea can be introduced slowly over time. Adopted children have the same rights as biological children. Adopted children may manifest unique genetic predispositions. Your adopted child may experience anxiety regarding possible abandonment issues as he is struggling to understand why he was given up for adoption. Your adopted child will need a great deal of loving reassurance. If a child is adopted by a family of a different race, there will be cultural adjustments to make. Be open and honest with your adopted child. Normalize the idea of adoption as much as possible. The major need will be for strong attachment and secure bonding that is based on love and trust. Adoptive parents will have to assist the adopted child to forge his own identity and help him discover his unique place in the world. A lot depends on the age of the adopted child and his specific history of possible trauma. The overall undertaking will be challenging. The adopted child may experience feelings of sadness and loss. He may be fearful of rejection. As the parent of an adopted child, be firm and loving. Help your child to become independent and well able to think for himself. Teach him a range of essential life skills. Provide him with many opportunities to express his feelings. Hug your adopted child often and reassure him that he will always be loved. Call his name with fondness.

Always keep your word. Sharing trivial information with your adopted child will help to build trust. Routines will add predictability to his life and serve to lower his anxiety level. Your adopted child will have many questions. As a parent, always be available. Let him know that he is special.

# GRANDPARENTS

Children who have access to good grandparents are fortunate. Good grandparents who have access to their grandchildren are blessed. As a parent, allow and encourage a strong bond between your child and his good grandparents. A good grandparent is always supportive of a good parent. A grandparent may offer advice but a grandparent should never assume the role of a parent. Parents and grandparents should always agree on management approaches. Consequences should be applied with consistency. There is a lot that a child can learn from his good grandparents. In addition to the joy that the relationship offers, your child will experience the older generation and learn about life in days past. In the case of a divorce, good grandparents may be a source of stability and nurturing. Grandparents must remember to set limits with their grandchildren even when they are having fun. Good grandparents may provide after school care and may help to tutor a grandchild. A good grandparent will help to instill good family values and good work habits in a grandchild. A good and close relationship with a grandchild will help that child to feel safe and secure in the world. Grandchildren love to hear stories about the past. A warm and nurturing relationship with a grandchild can help develop that child's coping skills and inner strength. The unconditional love of a grandparent will go a long way towards the development of a child's sense of self and his confidence. A good grandparent will inspire and support a grandchild with his projects. Good grandparents invest in their grandchildren. They will often fix special food and celebrate a grandchild's birthday in a grand way. Your child's overall physical and mental health will be enhanced through a loving relationship with his good grandparents. A good grandparent can be a certainty for your child.

# SINGLE PARENT FAMILIES

Single parenting can be challenging and stressful. Your child will pull you in many directions. Never take out your frustration on your child. It is important to establish routines and to remain organized. Every older child should be assigned a household chore. Everyone will have to play their roles. Plan carefully and stick to a budget. Explore all community resources for assistance including after-school programs and church sponsored events. Make sure that your child receives proper nutrition, adequate sleep, and daily exercise. Have your child get to bed early so that he can be up early enough to have breakfast. Get your child to school on time. The school social worker can be a great source of advice and support. Be firm and loving with your child. You will become frustrated at times. Do not yell at your child and do not hit your child. Apply reasonable consequences in a consistent manner. A time-out will help your child to feel bad for his inappropriate behaviors and help to build his conscience. Teach your child to know the difference between right and wrong. Emphasize self-control, kindness, and telling the truth. Help your child get into the habit of making good choices. Read to your child and have him read to you. Older siblings can help with homework and reading practice. Protect your child from risky people and live in a safe neighborhood if possible. Plan family events such as picnics and trips to the zoo. As a single parent, limit television and video games and supervise well. Let your child spend time outdoors, with supervision, where he can walk, run, and play in nature. As a single parent, join a support group and work cooperatively with other single parents in your community.

# BLENDED FAMILIES

A blended family is formed when two people come together and bring a child or children from previous relationships. It will take a great deal of time and patience to blend. There will be new people to get to know, and new people to enjoy and love. Parents should have a plan regarding parenting styles, values, and child management. Everyone should cultivate respect for privacy and social boundaries. Some members of the blended family may arrive with significant baggage caused by past traumas. Some members of the blended family may function with significant emotional problems that require professional intervention. Children in blended families will need to develop the skill of conflict resolution. Parents should not show favoritism and they should not compare the children. Everyone is different. What is fair should be based on need and not on want. The children in a blended family should keep competition to a minimum. As a parent, never accept disrespect, abuse, or violence. Train the children to respect both parents and to always be considerate of each other. Encourage communication, negotiation, and compromise. Have regular family meetings to spell out expectations and to discuss everyone's concerns.

# A GREAT FATHER

A great father is protective of his child. He is a great role model – respectful, loving, and supportive of mom. A great father is aware of his own functioning and aware of the impact he is having on his child. A great father exhibits good work habits and socially appropriate conduct at all times. He is patient, inspiring, warm, and controlled. A great father is a consistent and dependable provider. He is a calming influence and a major player in the management of his child. A great father is often engaged with his child in fun activities such as sports. A great father will help to supervise study time and reading practice. A great father will engage his child in daily conversations that will build his child's knowledge, vocabulary, and thinking skills. He will gladly attend school conferences to learn about ways to help his child. A great father will attend his child's school performances. A father is his daughter's first experience with the world of men. A loving and trusting relationship will boost his daughter's self-esteem and confidence. For his children, a great father is an example of responsibility and problem-solving ability. By words and by example, a great father teaches his son how to become a man. Having a great father in the life of a child reduces the chance of dropping out of school and experiencing conflict with the law. A great father is an example of open-mindedness and tolerance. He values his children as individuals and is unwavering in his love.

# A GREAT MOTHER

A great mother is protective of her child. She is nurturing, loving, and totally unselfish. A great mother is aware of her own functioning and aware of the impact she is having on her child. A great mother understands that her major role is to raise an independent and loving child who is fully capable of living in the real world. She understands the painful process of separation. A great mother is aware of her strengths and her deficits. She strives to be a healthy and happy person. A great mother is sensitive to the individual needs of every child and she is a creator of joy. She is patient and understanding. A great mother is consistent, forgiving, and calm. She is organized, affectionate, and flexible. A great mother never gives up on her child.

# STRONG AND ASSERTIVE

A s a parent, do not raise an aggressive child. Raise a child who is strong and assertive. Certainly, you do not want to raise a bully who is driven by an impaired conscience or by repressed rage. Model assertiveness. Do not allow others to take advantage of you. Say no when it is appropriate to say no. Do not be a weak, dependent follower. Do not commit to rigidly live up to any specific label. Be an independent thinker. Do not allow yourself to be victimized or bullied by anyone including family members. Do not allow friends, colleagues, and acquaintances to cross the line and treat you with a lack of respect. Teach your child to value and respect himself. Teach your child to speak up. The world is a tough place. People will take advantage of you if you allow them. Get in the habit of moving with strength and confidence when you are at home and when you are out in public. Excessive guilt and depression will prevent your child from being assertive and confident. From the beginning, instill in your child the principles of mutual respect, rights, and responsibility. Give your child choices and allow him to voice his opinions and disagreements. Involve your child in physical activities that will help him learn to be strong and assertive.

# WINNING AND LOSING

There is no greater feeling than winning after intense preparation and a strategic performance. All of us should strive to be winners. However, in real life we sometimes win and we sometimes lose. Teach your child to accept the outcome after giving his best effort. Sometimes you have to lose in order to win such as when you walk away from a confrontation before it escalates. When we compete, the little steps that lead us to an outcome are just as meaningful as winning. Enjoy the process of the game. Be happy for the person who wins and take the time to congratulate him. Winning requires ability and a lot of hard work. Confidence will take you far. Try to learn something from every defeat. When you compete, keep the interaction relaxed and cordial. When you are friendly to the opposition, your chance of winning increases. Winning is about ability, practice, mental toughness, and execution. You are always a winner when you give your best effort. Sometimes you win and sometimes you lose. Enjoy the game.

# HOW TO TALK TO YOUR CHILD

The ability to talk to a child is a gift. It helps if you really love children. Do not engage in baby talk. A young child understands a lot more than you think. Get down to your child's level and look him in the eye. Use simple language and speak with rhythm and clarity. Your voice should be soft and loving. Call your child by his name for his name is special. Have a serious conversation. Ask your child problem-solving questions. Ask your child for advice and for his opinions. Pause to allow time for your child to think and to formulate a response. Listen to your child. Do not fill his mind with scary thoughts and scary stories. Talk to your child about the positive things that are happening in the present. Praise your child for his verbal responses. Be gentle and warm with your requests. Talk about the weather. Talk about what is on the schedule. Talk about family plans. Talk about whatever your child wants to talk about.

# READINESS FOR THE
# STRUCTURE OF SCHOOL

A structured school program will contribute greatly to your child's overall development. At school he will be taught to follow rules and to follow a schedule. He will be exposed to a broad curriculum. Your child will learn to get along with other children who are different, and he will learn coping skills and conflict resolution. He will learn team work. Your child will learn to separate from you. As a parent, visit your child's teacher and your child's classroom before school begins. Make sure that your child understands that he should go to his teacher if there is a problem. School is an experience that will expose your child's strengths and deficits. He will be observed, discussed, and compared with other children. There are things you can do to prepare him for school. Do not pressure. Teach your child readiness skills in fun ways. Your child must be properly toilet trained. He must learn to be socially appropriate and he must learn to respect privacy and social boundaries. Your child must be compliant to adult authority and he must be able to follow simple directions. He should be able to sit still and complete a simple task. Your child should be able to listen to a simple question and produce an appropriate verbal response. He should be able to recognize letters, numbers, shapes, and colors, and be able to count to twenty. Your child should be able to color between the lines and use a pair of safety scissors to cut paper in a straight line. He should be able to eat his food independently and he should be able to name the days of the week. Teach your child about safety especially on the playground and in the parking lot. As a parent, you must be able to trust the classroom teacher to take care of your child. You will experience a great deal of anxiety when your child is away from you. The world is not a perfect place. We have to take some well calculated risks. Sending your child to school will contribute greatly to his overall development. Your job as a parent is to carefully prepare him for school and take measures to minimize the risks.

# LIVING IN THE REAL WORLD

I maginary and pretend activities will contribute greatly to your child's intellectual and emotional development. Through these activities your child will learn to visualize, reason, and develop compassion. When your child is about four years old, help him to establish a healthy balance between fantasy and reality. Talk to him about living in the real world. Make sure that your child is well oriented to time, person, and place. Teach your child to focus on the present. What is the weather like? How are you feeling right now? Teach your child that the real world offers adventure but at the same time significant risks. The trick to living in the real world is to take preventive measures, calculate the risks, and weigh the probability of disaster. It is about making good decisions. With your young child, do not over-emphasize evil and danger. These teachings will be appropriate when he is older. Teach your child about goodness, safety, and compliance. Your child must learn to stop himself. Do not instill unreasonable fear in your child. Health habits are important, such as washing your hands, but do not go overboard to the point of becoming germ phobic. Live in the real world. There is no magic. Coach your child into becoming an effective person who can make good things happen. Encourage your child to think for himself and to always make sense. Real life is a combination of joy and risk. Use the information that is available to you. Trust your intuition. Be observant, rational, and open-minded. Use your sound judgement to formulate your most accurate perception of reality. Have a feel for trends and patterns. Is the world becoming a more dangerous place? You cannot change the world to fit your child. You must prepare your child to live in the real world.

# BRAIN INJURY

One of your major jobs as a parent is to take measures to make sure that your child does not suffer a brain injury. Your child's brain can become injured from a blow to his head. He can become brain injured from falling from a high place or from an accident while travelling in a motor vehicle. A baby can experience brain injury through violent shaking. A closed head injury can take place when the soft and fragile brain tissue is slammed against the skull from a sudden and violent forward or backward movement. Children who suffer a brain injury may experience emotional problems, behavior problems, or learning problems. Make sure that your child wears protective gear while playing sports. Be sure that his seat belt is securely fastened when he is riding in a motor vehicle. Do not allow your child to be perched in high places. An amusement park ride that can give your child a major jolt is risky. Medical intervention should be sought for your child if he experiences a significant blow to his head that produces symptoms of neurological impairment such as loss of consciousness, dizziness, confusion, or severe headaches. Brain injury rehabilitation may include occupational therapy, speech and language therapy, and physical therapy. A child who suffers a brain injury will benefit from proper nutrition that will help heal his brain and from safety measures that will prevent a second brain injury from taking place.

# THE TEENAGE BRAIN

During the teenage years, the adolescent will experience significant brain growth. He will become more idealistic, more critical, and more philosophical. In many ways it will be a period of storm and stress. The teenager will face significant issues pertaining to body changes, independence, and career goals. The teenage brain is not sufficiently developed to handle the pressure. Teenagers lack maturity, sound judgement, and life experience. They are often self-absorbed and impulsive. Sometimes they are reckless, adventurous, and risk-taking. It is difficult for a teenager to delay gratification. Teenagers are not equipped to make major life decisions. As a parent, you must establish firm rules for your teenager who drives a motor vehicle. He must obey speed limits when he drives and he should always wear his seatbelt. Your teenager should not use his cell phone while driving. Wearing a helmet when riding a bicycle is a good habit. Encourage your teenager to self-evaluate, self-monitor, and self-regulate. Let your teenager know that the real pay-off for his hard work and discipline will come to him in the future. As a parent, it is your job to say no when it is appropriate to say no. Teach your teenager to respect the opposite sex and to be socially appropriate at all times. Your teenager is in the process of formulating his own beliefs and values. Encourage him to think for himself and to be open-minded and tolerant. Playing sports is a healthy outlet and an opportunity for your teenager to socialize with his peers. As a parent, it is your job to hold your teenager together until his teenage brain matures.

# HIDING BEHIND A
# MEDICAL DIAGNOSIS

It would not be difficult to obtain a medical diagnosis for your child. You may even receive a prescription to go with the medical diagnosis. Your child's problem may be physical. On the other hand, your child's problem may stem from his toxic parents or from experiencing emotional trauma. Many a parent would prefer to obtain a diagnosis of attention deficit hyperactive disorder rather than a diagnosis of stress disorder. An ADHD diagnosis would suggest that the parent is not the cause of the child's problem. It would also suggest that the child could be fixed by medication and without significant changes in the family structure and parenting style. If you are going to help your child, you will have to be honest with yourself. It will require a great deal of courage to come to terms with the impact you are having on your child. You may be required to make significant changes in the way you parent. Some parents distance themselves from the child's problems and hide behind a medical diagnosis. It is important to get to the root cause of your child's problems. Many parents feed their own fears, phobias, and anxieties to their children. Teach your child to obey. Teach your child to know the difference between right and wrong. Apply behavior consequences in a consistent manner. Teach your child to be socially appropriate, kind, and considerate. Help your child to develop conscience and help him learn to love and value himself. Teach your child to relax through the daily practice of quiet time. Teach your child impulse control and self-regulation. As a parent, take some responsibility for your child's problems and do not hide behind a medical diagnosis.

# GREAT TEACHERS

Great teachers have changed many lives. They are born to teach. A great teacher speaks with confidence and clarity like an actor on a stage. As you sit in their classrooms, you will be amazed at their poise, wit, and wisdom. Great teachers possess abundant enthusiasm and they are warm and loving. They explain things well and can produce concrete examples that bring learning to life. Great teachers are kind, caring, and patient. They love children and it shows. Great teachers respect children and are willing to individualize their approach to meet the needs of any child. A great teacher is firm and friendly and has a sense of humor. Creativity and organization are characteristics of a great teacher. A great teacher plans exciting projects for their students and is lavish with praise. They are fair with all concerned and respectful of everyone. Great teachers are bright and knowledgeable. When you sit in their classrooms, you will feel thrilled and warm all over. A great teacher will love and value your child.

# SUCCESS

Everyone has their own definition of success based on their unique beliefs, values, and philosophy of life. Some parents want their children to be healthy and happy. Some parents push their children to excel in school. Some people define success in terms of accumulating wealth. Whatever your definition of success, it will require skills, hard work, and confidence to succeed. As a parent, you must individualize your approach to your child based on his strengths and his interests. If you apply too much pressure, your child will break. If you parent with love and firmness, your child will achieve. If you are a "do nothing" permissive parent, your child will grow up to be a weakling. If you are a high anxiety parent, your child will grow up to be frightened. Your goals for your child should include good health, independent functioning, creativity, and involvement in meaningful work. Teach your young child to sit still and complete an age-appropriate task. Help him to follow a daily schedule. Teach your child a range of essential life skills through family activities and help him to function with independence. To become successful in life, your child must know the difference between right and wrong. He must learn to follow rules and learn to respect authority. Your child must respect privacy and social boundaries. It is more important to raise a kind, loving child with a well-developed conscience than to raise an intellectually gifted person who is evil. Your child must know that he is loved and valued. The formula for success is ability combined with hard work.

# TRUST

It is important that your child feel safe and secure in the world. As a parent, always be consistent and predictable with your child. Keep your word when you make a promise to him. Trust between people is increased when there is self-disclosure. Share trivial information with your child. Tell him what you did and what you saw today. Tell him how it all made you feel. Slowly introduce your child to reality. There is much to learn. Your child must understand that there are good people and bad people in the world. Let your older child know about danger. It will raise his anxiety level but that is much better than having to face a tragedy. For a young child, the topics of death, crime, and natural disasters can wait. Train your child to obey you promptly and never to wander away from the safety of home and the safety of his parents. He must never go with strangers. Your child must be properly supervised at all times. Sleepovers are a major risk. Emphasize safety to your child in regards to parked cars, parking lots, driveways, and swimming pools. Trusting everyone is not a realistic and safe idea. Tell your child often that you love him and that he is special. Let him know that you will always take care of him and protect him. As he gets older teach him to trust his sensible intuition.

# TEACH YOUR CHILD TO READ

Read to your baby every day starting before he is born. Read simple, happy stories that teach a good lesson. Let your voice be soft and soothing. Have fun as you teach your child to read. With time, your child will form a connection between reading books and having fun. As your child grows older and can focus, point out pictures to him while you describe the picture. This is picture reading. Introduce an older child to simple books with a few words and large pictures. Let him tell you about the picture he is looking at. He can also make up a story about the picture. You can then have your child draw a picture of the story. Improve your child's visual memory by having him recall pictures that were shown to him. You can make up flash cards of interesting objects for visual memory drills. An older child may be ready to learn the names of the letters of the alphabet. You can then get him to practice naming the letters when he sees them. When he is ready, teach your child the sounds of the alphabet letters. Make a short game of it. You may wish to sing the alphabet letters as a song. The key to reading is visual recognition and sounding out letters and words. Your child must first learn to recognize a letter and then sound it out. The next step is to sound out simple words such as cat and bat. Make flash cards of word families for practice. Have your child read to you as soon as he can read simple words and sentences. This will help him to build confidence.

Praise him for his reading. Cuddle your child as you read to him. Then, let him read to you while he is snuggled on your lap. His reading will improve with daily practice. Soon he will be a great reader.

# PET OR NO PET

Getting a pet is a major family decision. There are benefits and there are risks. Having a gentle pet may reduce your stress and may help you to relax. Having a dog around the house may increase your personal sense of safety. Cuddling a pet may make you feel happy and secure. Caring for a pet can be an experience in giving and receiving love. A pet can be a good companion for your child. When you get a pet, you are giving an animal a home. On the other hand, having a pet is a great deal of responsibility and cost. Your vet is not in love with you and your pet. It is all business. Engaging in spontaneous activities away from home will be more difficult when you have a pet. Who in the family will be caring for the pet? Getting a pet is a commitment for the life of the pet. As your pet gets older it will require more care. Some pets are unpredictable and cannot be trusted to be around children. Some people are allergic to their pets. Are you and your children prepared for the fact that your pet will eventually die? Getting a pet is a big decision.

# EDUCATION CHANGES
# OVER TIME

E ducational philosophies come and go. In years past, teachers
taught a basic curriculum and then took off on topics and
projects that were interesting and relevant to students. Back
then, there was more local control of education. Teachers and
students spent a great deal of time outdoors. Learning was fun
and children looked forward to going to school. Teachers involved
their students in bug and rock collecting and a variety of art
projects. Some teachers made applesauce with their students and
then gave them writing assignments about making applesauce.
Raising butterflies and tadpoles and planting gardens were
other activities that students and teachers engaged in. Brighter
students assisted the students who were less capable. Students
went on field trips and some students observed objects under
a microscope. With time, education became more centralized,
more controlled, and more technological. Schools need to be the
fun and safe place they used to be.

# AN OVER-STIMULATED CHILD

Your child may be overwhelmed by excessive stimulation. Within the normal environment there is a great deal of movement. People and pets are everywhere. The country is lighted up night and day. Cars go back and forth. People work around the clock. Some stores are open all night. Families are busy with household duties, television, and video games. Everyone seems to be in a frenzy. We accumulate a bunch of things that we do not need. We are always in a rush because there is too much to do. For your child's sake, slow it down. Relax. Keep it simple. Protect your child from adult concerns. Make sure that your child has his own bed to sleep in. The child who is experiencing sensory overload may be tense and stressed. His sleep may be disturbed. The child who is experiencing excessive stimulation may engage in a range of poor behaviors. A young child may cry or become cranky. Relax and enjoy some quiet time with your child. Have him lie on a blanket and enjoy some relaxing time for ten minutes. Cuddle your child as you enjoy some quiet time. While it is essential to stimulate your child's five senses—sight, sound, taste, smell, and touch—the over-stimulation of your child is detrimental. As a parent, strive to keep it simple. All good things in moderation.

# CONFLICT WITH THE LAW

As a parent, do all that you can to make sure that your child does not have to experience the hell of prison which is more about revenge than about rehabilitation. Be a good example. Obey the laws of society. Have nothing to do with illicit drugs and do not drink and drive. Always be fair and reasonable. Have your child practice impulse control. There are many people in prison today because they were not able to control their rage. Let your child know that the police officers are here to serve and protect the community. Let your child know that he should be soft-spoken, respectful, and compliant if he ever encounters the police. Help your child to develop a conscience and learn to respect rules and adult authority. As a parent, apply consequences in a consistent manner. Train your child to take responsibility for his behaviors and choices. A measure of guilt enhances conscience. A ten-minute time out is a good idea for bad behaviors. Praise all good behaviors. Teach your child about rights, privacy, personal space, and boundaries. As a parent, do not allow violence or any other type of abuse in your home. Let your child express himself with the use of his words. By teaching and by example, teach your child to be kind, caring, controlled, and peaceful. Teach your child to walk away from confrontation before it escalates. Never teach your child that the world is against him. Teach your child to avoid bad people. Keep your child focused on academics, music, and sports. Your child may benefit from joining a church group. Teach values to your child every day. Talk about a good community and talk about a good life now and in the future. Value freedom and do not let your child enter the hell of prison.

# SCHOOL INVOLVEMENT

Some parents are difficult. Some teachers are difficult. A parent-teacher relationship should be based on mutual respect. As a parent, never let your child hear you speak negatively about his teacher. A parent and a teacher must present a united front. It is a good sign when your child's teacher invites you to visit the classroom. Such an invitation should be interpreted as an indication of their competence and confidence. Sit down with the classroom teacher to discuss any concerns regarding your child. Seek to understand the teacher's philosophy of education and teaching. As a parent, your biggest need is for reassurance that your child will be safe at school and that he will be treated with kindness and fairness. It is also a good sign when the classroom teacher invites you to help supervise students on field trips and on other special occasions. From the beginning, establish a system of communication with the teacher. Over-involvement on the part of a parent may create dependency on the part of a child. Never ask to attend school to sit at your child's side. Discuss with the classroom teacher ways to help your child on the home front.

# ACADEMIC ACHIEVEMENT

A cademic skills are developed mostly through structured learning which is highly dependent on instruction and practice. The best predictor of academic achievement is intelligence, which reflects both incidental and structured learning. As a parent, make sure that your child attends school every day so that he does not miss the sequence of instruction and become disconnected from his class. Make sure that your child has breakfast before going to school. In addition to intellectual ability, your child must have good work habits and a strong desire to achieve. At home, teach your child to sit still and complete a given task in a specific amount of time. Help your child to develop good concentration by having him listen to and repeat back a series of random numbers. Help your child to develop strong visual memory by recalling objects, letters, or numbers that were shown to him. Academic achievement may also be enhanced by improving your child's visual reasoning ability with the use of visual patterns and pictures. Your child should strive to become a good phonetic reader. Have your child practice his phonics by reading a list of nonsense words. As a parent, you can improve your child's fine motor performance through the timed copying of letters and numbers. Work with your child on abstract vocabulary such as above and below. Teach your child to follow a schedule and to be organized. Academic achievement is highly dependent on having proper sleep, healthy nutrition, pure water, and daily exercise. Train your child to be independent. Encourage him to complete his school assignments on his own. Use flash cards and the computer for additional academic practice. Always praise your child for his academic achievement.

# CONDUCT DISORDER/
# EMOTIONAL IMPAIRMENT

Conduct disorder, in your child, is often the result of poor socialization and failure to develop age-appropriate social skills. Conduct disorder may be a direct result of inadequate parenting and your child's failure to develop a conscience. Many children who exhibit conduct disorder are impulsive, disruptive and aggressive. Emotional impairment exists when your child is handicapped in his thinking, mood, and behavior by negative emotions such as fear, sadness, anxiety, or anger. Emotional impairment is often caused by emotional trauma.

# WORKING PARENTS

In more than half of all families, both parents work outside the home. Juggling a job and child-rearing is challenging but not impossible. We know that babies thrive with warm, loving, dedicated caregivers. On the other hand, attachment and bonding may be interrupted when both parents work. One or both parents may experience anxiety, sadness, or guilt. Families will have to plan well. Everyone will have to play their roles. Household duties will have to be divided. Older children will have to assist the younger ones. Proper time management will be important. Following a schedule will be essential. Weekends and holidays will have to count. Children may experience significant fear and loneliness when their parents are away. They may have too many responsibilities. Never leave young children alone without supervision. Parents will have to contend with hectic evenings, loss of sleep, and fatigue. With both parents working, it will be important to have regular family meetings to plan. Communication will be vital. Allow all family members to express their concerns. Parents may wish to explain to their children the reasons why they work. It is often about financial security, contributing to the world, and experiencing fulfillment. Parents will have to work hard to coordinate family life. Accept all the help that is available from extended family and friends.

# BELIEFS AND FACTS

Help your older child to understand the difference between a belief and a fact. A belief is an opinion or thought that a person regards as true. A belief may be based on indoctrination, personal experience, or science. A belief may or may not be rational or factual. A fact is an objective truth that is provable through scientific evidence. For example, the earth is round. Many times, in the absence of facts, we have beliefs. A person can choose to believe anything, but you cannot wish a scientific fact away. An important part of your child's development is the refinement of his beliefs as he grows older. As a parent, have conversations with your child. Be a good listener. Do not be controlling and rigid. Allow your child the freedom to change his beliefs. A good belief is that humans are inherently valuable. A bad belief is that people are poor because they are inherently stupid and lazy. Be careful about what you believe because beliefs will lead to feelings, and feelings will lead to actions. In order to change your behavior, you have to change your belief. Do not over indoctrinate your child with your beliefs. Let him become his own person. Encourage your child to think for himself. There is a lot that we do not know.

# YOUR CHILD'S INTERESTS
# AND PASSIONS

As a parent, take the time to explore and nurture your child's interests and passions. Expose him to a variety of experiences. Let him try new activities. If your child enjoys reading, you can establish a book fund so that he will have new books to read. Your child may be mechanically inclined. Involve him in projects around the house. Let him help you fix things. Your child may be athletic and interested in playing sports. Purchase some sports equipment and practice with him. Train him to run. Have him learn to throw a ball. Have him learn to catch a ball. He may be ready to play on a team. If your child is interested in music, buy him a musical instrument. Surely you can endure some noisy drums for the sake of your child. He may be interested in art. Buy him some art supplies and encourage him to draw. If your child is interested in learning to cook, teach him the basics of safety in the kitchen and allow him to assist you until he is old enough to fix some simple dishes on his own. You can start with making a sandwich. Some children enjoy discussions and debate. Involve them in daily conversations. If your child is extroverted, he may be interested in acting. Let him perform small acting parts to entertain the family. Your child may be interested in collecting coins. Purchase a few coin folders and help him get started. Some children grow up to be great thinkers and creators of ideas. Help your child with the basics of writing prose or writing poetry. Some children love plants. Give your child some garden space and help him acquire a few plants. If your child is interested in animals, you may consider getting a pet. He may enjoy a visit to the zoo. As your child gets older, he may become excited over science, math, or history. Encourage him. Do not hesitate to share your child's interests and passions with his classroom teacher.

# PASSIONATE VISUALIZATION

Most of our waking hours are spent processing visual information. With time, your child will become a strong visual learner. Encourage him to hold a visual image in his mind and experience it with great passion. Take your child on many scenic trips. Encourage him to picture in his mind the scenes that he reads about. Your child may choose to hold a relaxing scene in his mind of a place he has visited. Encourage him to visualize happy events and interesting places with great passion. Let your child visualize success with great passion. Have him close his eyes and passionately visualize physical activity such as walking, running, or playing a sport. Encourage him to picture himself living a great life of creativity and of benefit to humanity. Encourage your child to visualize himself as well behaved and peaceful. Teach him to visualize a peaceful scene such as the ocean, a sunset, or a beautiful garden so that he can relax and have a calm mind. Encourage your child to enjoy the beauty that is in the natural world.

# RELIGION AND YOUR CHILD

Religious teaching may be good for your child but be careful not to over indoctrinate. Emphasize to your child the importance of living a life that is full of love, kindness, and tolerance. Religion can be a source of moral training and the development of values. Put the emphasis on good behaviors, taking care of the environment, and lending a helping hand to the poor, the sick, and the aged. Religious music may help to relax your child's mind. As your child matures, he may develop religious beliefs that are different from yours. Encourage him to think for himself and to adopt beliefs that are kind, rational, and realistic. Let him know that you do not have all the answers. Religion may make you feel safe, secure, and hopeful. Teach your child to respect and value other people's religion. Encourage your child to live by the Golden Rule. Do unto others what you would like them to do unto you. Religious training is good for your child when the emphasis is on living a life full of love, kindness, and tolerance.

# THE AMERICAN DREAM

The American dream is a belief that anyone, regardless of where they were born, can attain upward mobility in America if they are willing to work hard. The American dream has been defined in terms of material success – education, job, and money. There are many opportunities in America if one is willing to make the effort and abide by the rules. As a parent, instill in your child the desire not just to take but also to give back to the community. It should always be our goal to do our part to contribute to the improvement of society. The definition of the American dream needs to be skillfully personalized and expanded. Encourage your child to take responsibility. Teach him to think for himself so that he does not become a follower or a victim. Let the American dream include the pursuit of health and joy. Teach your child to extend kindness and tolerance to all people. Those who have achieved the American dream should lend a helping hand to the less fortunate. Live a simple, low stress life. Help your child to develop conscience as part of the American dream and encourage him not to become obsessed with material possessions.

# YOUR CHILD
# AND SOCIAL MEDIA

Social media should be recognized as a major socialization agent. There are some benefits. Through social media there can be collaboration, social learning, and connectivity. On the other hand, as a parent, you need to warn your child that he can become the victim of negative behaviors and destructive feedback from others on social media. Your child must learn to say no to bullying and walk away. Social media can also become an addiction and a major distraction from your child's academic achievement. As a parent, it is your job to set the limits and to supervise well.

# YOUR CHILD AND ALLERGIES

Y our child's sleep difficulty, low energy, behavior disorder, and learning problems may have something to do with allergies. While your child may be showing signs of stress, it is possible that he is exhibiting allergic reactions to his environment or to his food. If your child continues to experience difficulty over an extended period of time, you should consult his pediatrician to explore the possible impact of allergies.

# SELF-DEFEATING BEHAVIORS

Take the time to introduce the concept of self-defeating behaviors to your older child. Let him know that his choices have consequences. Explain to your older child the many ways in which he can sabotage himself. It is self-defeating for your child to neglect his physical and mental health—especially exercise and sleep. Excessive self-criticism is self-defeating. Teach your child to understand reality and to value scientific evidence. Being rigid and perfectionistic creates excessive stress. Your child should never compare himself to others. He should not allow social withdrawal to become a pattern in his life. Accept help when help is needed. Many opportunities will come your child's way. He needs to grab them. Tell your child never to engage in reckless behaviors such as drug or alcohol use. Encourage him to be selective with his friends. It is always self-defeating when you repeat the same mistake. Failure to take responsibility and always blaming others are also self-defeating patterns. Negative thinking may lead to depression. Procrastination, disorganization, and escaping into the world of the internet are self-defeating. Attention seeking behaviors are also self-defeating in the end. It is self-defeating to allow irrational fear to dominate your life. Let your child know that his negative emotions will create a blockage to the free flow of his positive energy.

# FAMILY WITH A
# HANDICAPPED CHILD

Raising a handicapped child is challenging. There will be enormous stress on everyone in the family. As a parent, you may experience feelings of depression and anger. Having a handicapped child can trigger a grieving process for the perfect child that you do not have. You may go through periods of denial and periods of resentment. You may experience guilt and you may experience significant fear and anxiety. Siblings may be confused regarding the enormous attention and effort that caring for your handicapped child demands. There may be enormous costs involved. There might be significant disruption to family life. Schedule special time for each child. It will be important to have regular family meetings to discuss family matters and the specific concerns of all the children. The goal should be to have a normal existence as much as possible. Be sure to celebrate each child's achievements and milestones. As a parent of a handicapped child, have a social support system in place. You may need to take breaks now and then. Cultivate your physical and emotional health. Having a handicapped child can be stressful on a marriage. Be a team and work as a team.

# TELEVISION AND YOUR CHILD

Television is a powerful medium which can be educational and inspiring. It may serve to enhance your child's thinking skills. Your child may become interested in exploring topics he has viewed. Television may improve your child's social skills and help him to become more aware of his feelings. Television offers the benefits of cultural exposure, family fun, and entertainment. It may help to relieve your child's stress and increase his language skills and creativity. Your child may become interested in playing sports after watching sports on television. On the other hand, your child can become addicted to television. It can rob him of valuable time for academics, social interactions, creative activities, and outdoor exercise. Your child may be exposed to poor values, violence, and adult topics. Television may give your child a distorted view of reality. As a parent, take the time to discuss television content with your child and answer his questions. It is your job to help select wholesome television programs for your child. Supervise well and set limits.

# INTERVENTION

No matter how hard you try, your child will have some physical, mental, or emotional problems. Always be cautious when you are selecting an intervention program. Medication and hospitalization are last resort interventions. Consultation and counseling are less drastic. As a parent, you should consider a mild intervention program for a start. Be sure that you are well informed before giving your consent for treatment. Keep in mind that psychiatric diagnostic labels are what humans subjectively invented. Your child's diagnosis may or may not be accurate. Think it through carefully. Keep in mind that drugs have adverse side effects. On the other hand, there are many caring and competent professionals available to you. Choose wisely. Read the reviews. Evaluate progress over time and change course if it becomes necessary. If a professional is disrespectful to you, find someone else to help you with your child. As a parent, there must be a good fit between the professional you select and you, the parent. There must also be a good fit between the professional you select and your child.

# STICK TO THE BASICS

The world is a combination of joy and pain, risks and rewards. As you parent your child, you will have to take well calculated risks. You will have to trust someone. There will be a lot of scary information coming at your child from a variety of sources. He will be frightened and he will be overwhelmed. His sleep may be disturbed and he may function with heightened anxiety. Help your child to manage his stress. Involve him in daily exercise, daily conversations, and quiet time. Encourage your child to express himself through words, music, and sports. Teach him to use positive self-talk. Teach your child to relax. Teach him social skills. Have your child spend time in nature. Practice impulse-control with your child. Help him refine and further develop his motor skills through physical activity. By teaching and by example, train your child to be kind and compassionate. Create many social experiences and great memories for your child. Teach him many essential life skills. Help your child to construct a day's schedule and learn to follow it. Encourage him to live his life in blocks of time. A child with skills is a confident child. Get him ready to live in the real world. There is no magic. It takes dedication and it takes hard work. Stick to the basics.

# COUNT YOUR BLESSINGS

Quit complaining so much. Instead, count your many blessings. Cultivate gratitude. Do not simply feel thankful. Say "thank you" to the many wonderful people who are kind to you. It is easy to focus on the negative side of life when you are sad, angry, or frightened. Get in the habit of engaging in positive but realistic thinking. Be thankful for good friends and family. Be thankful for your food, your job, and your home. Be thankful for the beauty of nature. Be thankful for the ones who love you. Be thankful for all the people who helped you along the way. Be thankful for your health. Put life in perspective. Think about what you have instead of what you do not have. Count your blessings.

# UNHEALTHY HOMES/
# UNHEALTHY SCHOOLS

Your child's functioning will be greatly influenced by the healthiness of his home and the healthiness of his school. A child raised in a troubled family will have behavioral and emotional problems. Some unhealthy patterns within a family include a lack of structure and organization, aggression, poor impulse control, and low frustration tolerance. Some unhealthy family systems function with unclear social boundaries and with too much or too little control. Within an unhealthy family system, a child may experience more failure than success. He may be called bad or stupid. Within an unhealthy family system, a child may not be taught appropriate social skills, and he may be exposed to parents who manipulate others. He may experience few successes and limited play time. Within an unhealthy family system, a child may not learn to deal effectively with his emotions and with his frustrations. The next influential system is school. Do not underestimate the impact that school will have on your child. In the first place, there may be a discrepancy between the philosophy of home and the philosophy of school. The classroom teacher may be punitive, distant, incompetent, disorganized, and unloving. Your child may be the target of bullying by his classmates. He may experience failure because of the teacher's inability to individualize your child's instruction. Some of your child's classmates may be aggressive and threatening. Your child's overall development will be highly influenced by the healthiness of his home and the healthiness of his school.

# EMOTIONALLY AVAILABLE
# TO YOUR CHILD

The emotional development of your child may be your most important task and your greatest accomplishment. As a parent, be emotionally available to your child. Engage with him and stay in the present. Give your child your undivided attention when you interact with him. Share your feelings with your child as you engage him on matters that are age appropriate and pertinent. Do not involve your child with weighty adult concerns. Always acknowledge his feelings and let him know that you understand how he feels. Reassure him that you care and that you love him. Let him know that you are proud of him. Call his name frequently and give him hugs and backrubs. Listen to your child without judgement. Share trivial information about your day. It will build trust. Encourage your child to share his feelings and give him the opportunity to do so. As a parent, be emotionally alive and schedule daily "love time" with your child.

# RAISING A
# RESPONSIBLE CHILD

There is no magic and there is no specific formula. As a parent, it is better to adopt a democratic system instead of an authoritarian or permissive approach to your child. Be willing to give your older child some choices and be willing to negotiate and compromise. Humans form habits easily. It is your job to mold your child towards a sense of responsibility. There are some basics that should be in place. Your child must know the difference between right and wrong and he must develop conscience. He must learn to be compliant and he must be able to control his impulses. Your child must learn to respect adult authority. Allow your child to become independent by making him responsible for the completion of age-approach tasks and chores. When you do everything for your child, you are teaching him to become dependent and helpless. Teach your child to be considerate of others. Social skills are important. Your child must know what is expected of him. Help him to cultivate a healthy balance between work and play. Teach your older child about rights, privacy, and boundaries. He must learn the difference between needs and wants and learn to delay gratification. Structure is important for any child. Teach him to follow a schedule. Teach your child to solve problems. Instead of begging your child, use a firm but loving voice to make your request known. Praise your child's good behaviors. A negative consequence such as a time out, loss of television time, or an early bedtime should be applied to poor behaviors. Be consistent with consequences. You raise a responsible child by making him responsible for his chores, his school-work, and his behavior. Emphasize the concept that we are a family. We do not blame. When something goes wrong, we fix it. As a parent, you teach your child to be responsible by being a model of responsibility.

# DO NOT TRY TO
# SAVE THE WORLD

As a parent, do the best that you can. Learn as much as you can. Do not try to save the world. Live in the world the way the world is. There is not a whole lot that is negotiable. Never try to apply simple solutions to life's complex problems. There is a lot that we do not know. Be happy with yourself for making a small difference in the world. Focus on your child. Be able to recite his strengths and his passions. Know what works for him and know what does not work for him. Your goal is to raise an intelligent, creative, independent, productive child with a tremendous capacity to love. You do not have to be a perfect parent to raise a good citizen. Give your child many positive experiences and great memories. Strive to protect your child from physical and emotional trauma. Teach your child to know the difference between right and wrong and help him to develop a conscience. Have daily conversations with your child and let him express his thoughts and feelings. Teach your child to be socially appropriate at all times. Encourage your child to become a strong visual learner. Train him to think for himself. Your best gift to your child is a healthy, happy, and relaxed you. Do not try to save the world. Save your child. If you do not save your child, no one else will. If you should lose your child, none of your accomplishments will ever compensate for your great loss. If you save your child, he will be your greatest gift to the world.

# THE POWER OF YOUR UNCONDITIONAL LOVE

As a parent, you must be willing to die for your child. In the final analysis, love is what you do. Love is not effortless. Love is effortful. The love between a good parent and a child has no limits and no conditions. The bond between a good parent and a child cannot be broken. Your child's pain will be the most gut-wrenching pain that you will ever experience. Unconditional love demands that you love your child when he is well and when he is sick. It requires you to love your child when he succeeds and when he fails. Unconditional love demands that you love your child when he adopts beliefs that are different from your beliefs. The unconditional love of a parent will support a child in his choice of career, his areas of interest, and his sexual orientation. The unconditional love of a parent demands that you facilitate your child's separation from you into a life of independent functioning. There should be no terms and there should be no conditions. Accept your child for the person he is. Value your child's uniqueness and special qualities. As a parent, cultivate unconditional love so that you have something pure and precious to give. Through the power of your unconditional love, your child will fall in love with himself. Through the power of your unconditional love, a therapeutic alliance will be forged between you and your child.

CPSIA information can be obtained
at www.ICGtesting.com
Printed in the USA
LVHW032324280423
745610LV00001B/84

9 781977 262080